# THE STEPPING-STONE OF GOD:
## CREATION

FINTAN CREAVEN

# The Stepping-Stone of God: Creation

## Earth-bound Spirituality

ST PAULS

ST PAULS
Middlegreen, Slough SL3 6BT, United Kingdom
Moyglare Road, Maynooth, Co. Kildare, Ireland

© ST PAULS (UK) 1995

Cover by MaryLou Winters; photo by Helena Madden

ISBN 085439 497 4

Printed by The Guernsey Press Co. Ltd, Guernsey, C.I.

ST PAULS is an activity of the priests and brothers of the
Society of St Paul who proclaim the Gospel through the media
of social communication

# Contents

# Introduction

*Finding my stance*

The other night I watched some figure skating on Television. It was a competition and was won, convincingly by those wonderful skaters, Torvill and Dean. Ten years previously they had swept the board with their rendering of 'Bolero' and now they had come up with an interpretation of 'Let's Sing and Dance'. The piece of music seemed to be all important. It really mattered which piece of music they decided to interpret. They had to dance to some tune, and they had to find the tune that enabled them to express their skill most completely.

I have come to the conclusion that something similar is true of our own lives, and our spiritual lives in particular. There is plenty of music around, yet we have to find the tune that suits us, the tune that best allows us to express what is in us, a tune that we can really dance to. If we try to accommodate ourselves to too many tunes we fail to express anything, and spend our time falling about the ice! Yet obviously we can also become too rigid and typified.

We need, then, to take a stance.

What do I mean by this? There are many ways to God, many spiritualities. Different traditions have described different ways. Obviously it will help to find one that suits. Yet it is not so much a 'spirituality' that I refer to as a 'stance' in life. I mean an outlook on the world. The story of the Secret Garden says this very well. As long as the three were set in a negative mode they were cramped and disabled. When they broke out of that, and discovered their 'tune' they began to dance.

So, at the outset, do what St Ignatius recommends at the beginning of the second week of the Spiritual Exercises. Pretend you are standing with the Holy Trinity looking from above down onto the world. What do you see? A world at odds with itself? A mixture, no doubt, of good and bad. You see two opposite forces at work, things combining and growing bigger, states joining to become bigger units like the EEC, empires being established, but also fragmenting, breaking into smaller nations under the force of nationalism and separatism. You find the emphasis being put on the individual in some cases, on the group in others.

Ignatius' meditation certainly saw the bad: people running leather for hell, as you might say. What is my view? What do I see? Do I think I am in a basically good or bad world? A lot depends on my viewpoint, on my stance. Is it good or bad? It is both. Which do I stress? My whole spirituality will depend on it.

God saw that it was GOOD. Yet there is obviously so much that is bad. We have inherited a point of view that distrusts the goodness of creation and sees it as primarily bad, needing to be redeemed to goodness.

Yet God created in his own image...

If the world were not good, if it were merely a corridor into something further, it could be easily discounted. Only a world that means a great deal to its creator is worth dying for.

Why should we bother? Why work for a kingdom on earth, when in fact we are headed for heaven? Does it really MATTER what we do here, except prepare our souls for the next life?

There are two possible ways of considering our time on earth. Is it a testing time for heaven? Or is it a time to work with God in the building of creation? Again it comes down to our and God's outlook on creation. If it is a basically bad thing, to be avoided, then life will seem to be a testing time.

Is our life then a sort of exam which we must pass in order to get into heaven? When we sit an exam the papers are there to test us, and once the test is done they are useless. They are not sold as literature afterwards, nor are they of value in themselves but only as ways of proving our ability to pass the exam.

If this is our life, an exam, then we have to earn our way to eternal life, we have to gain enough brownie points to get into the University of Heaven. We are allowed in on the basis of how we have done in our living on earth.

To this way of thinking earth-values in their own right are non-existent, they are only there to test us. The monks in the desert used to weave baskets, as occupational therapy, on Mondays, and unweave them on Tuesdays. The baskets in themselves (in the view of the monks) were useless except to keep them occupied in the making. Earth has no value in itself, but only as a test for us. In fact, earth is a trap. It is put there to be avoided, to provide the necessary temptations which we have to avoid if we are to pass the exam. Earth things are the 'catch questions' put there to enable us to avoid them. The world is transitory, being material, and hence not the basis for trust. Only eternal verities last, all our view should be towards eternity like a captain looking to the horizon, not into the water under the keel. We are birds of passage, migrants, not settling here, but stopping for a brief while on our way to our permanent home. Our time is a test, survived only by the fittest. The others perish, drawn aside, like the Argonauts, by the false beauty of the goods of this chimeric land.

Subtly intertwined in this view is an underlying assumption or rather, suspicion, that material things are not to be trusted, are not good. Only spiritual things are truly good. To attain to God and the things of God is a process of trying, impossibly, to strip away material things and to concentrate only on that which is spiritual. Hence asceticism is seen as the path to holiness. All human effort which

9

is aimed at the betterment of this earth is, at root, considered to be materialistic. It is like putting your trust in doing the exam rather than gaining the degree!

This has led to a view that Christians are not really interested in such material pursuits as politics, business and the use of power. Of course, it hasn't stopped them, but it has left them feeling that only half their life (the churchy half) is really Christian, the rest is earthly.

Hence the Christian is suspected of not being interested in the human effort. At best it is occupational therapy, the exam. The terms of the exam, the subjects, the syllabus, are relatively unimportant. Who remembers the answer to 'if it takes three men 4 hours to dig a hole 5 feet long and 3 feet wide and 6 feet deep how long will it take five men to dig one 6 feet long and 4 feet wide and 5 feet deep...?' Undertakers perhaps?

This way of thinking is prevalent, and leads to 'exam nerves', to guilt feelings, to 'swotting' in the sense of trying to store up treasure to carry us through. It is other-worldly in outlook, it is always future-orientated, never based on the worthwhileness of the here and now. Its 'other-world' nature however is a bit deceptive, because it is really a storing up treasure transferred from here to there. ('Treasure is treasure, dammit, whether here or in heaven!' *Franny & Zooey* by Salinger.)

The effect on the life of a person dedicated to this point of view is sensed by the poet R.S. Thomas in his radio poem, *The Minister* in the summing up by the Narrator as he says that our religion can be

– the adroit castrator
Of art; the bitter negation
Of song and dance and the heart's innocent joy –
You have botched our flesh and left us only the soul's
Terrible impotence in a warm world.

And the Narrator continues:

   – for he chose to fight
   With that which yields to nothing human.
   He never listened to the hills'
   Music calling to the hushed
   Music within.

Peering into the 'Beyond' prevents the seeker from finding the God who is present in creation. To find that God we need, as another poet, Rilke, says, to 'learn earthliness', a true sense of God's grace reaching out to us through the earth itself.

In order to avoid the distortions of a heaven-based rather than an earth-based spirituality, Juan Luis Segundo SJ proposed the model of 'God's Project'. God is involved with the world, he wants the development of creation and its final renewal and glory. His kingdom, his project, is the building up of the creation according to his desire, his love, planted there. This gives worth and value to the work we do here and now in helping to build the kingdom. The things of earth are not useless, what we do here is of value, as Teilhard saw, because we are building the kingdom of God. Thy will be done on earth as in heaven.

We are invited by Christ, called, to enter into this project and help build the kingdom. This calls for great unselfishness, willingness to serve. This service is for our fellow men and women. It implies a real use of our talents which are God-given, rather than a repressing of them in the interests of 'mortification', the killing of the body to 'liberate' the spirit, a dualistic idea. Our inner spirit is beckoned, as T.S. Eliot puts it, to quicken to the created world.

We are called to join our brothers and sisters in this work, not just within our own religious order, or church, or country, but with all people in a crusade to respect creation, because it is of God, and God is in it. God the creator wants us to be creators in our turn, to his glory. To help you to meditate on God's presence in our creation take the text of the Jacob's Dream (Genesis 28:10-19). Reflect on the importance of the place and on Jacob's words: 'God really is present in this place and I didn't even realise it!'

Or pray with the text of Elijah's journey to Horeb (1 Kings 19:4-19) and his experience of God in the gentle breeze.

# CHAPTER I

# The God-Source

*God appeared to Abraham at the oak of Mamre*
*as he sat by his tent in the heat of the day.*
*Looking up he saw three men standing near him...*

Christians have always seen in this story a vision of God himself. It is portrayed in an icon of the Trinity by Rublev. Sit or kneel before this picture and let your gaze wander round it. As you contemplate it you are drawn into the life of the three persons, Father, Son and Spirit.

There is no sign here of the old bearded patriarch depicted in many a painting of God. This is a family at table, sitting in contemplative serenity around the cup of the Eucharist, blessed by the gesture of their hands. Ageless and youthful, eternal and beautiful, the heads are inclined each to the other in loving deference, I-Thou, I-Thou, I-Thou. Contained here is all the passion of a lover for the loved one, the care of a parent for a child, and all the dedication of a person for a life-long friend.

It is a tapestry of similarity and opposites, woven into one: rest and movement, youth and maturity, restraint and pity, eternity and history, equality in difference.

It seems to be so complete a circle, so impenetrable! Yet at the front there is a place for you, the observer, and behind the heads you can see a house and a tree, representing creation. Love, like the Big Bang that threw the universe into being, is ever expanding. It cannot be held in, but must be shared. God created the cosmos as an expression of love, which glows outwards at this moment into creation, and is present in every atom. Created things take their meaning from the life of God. They are created for the glory of God. Aside from him they have no meaning.

Once creation comes into existence there is no longer a detached, unaffected and unchangeable God. God created out of love, the Son became incarnate out of love, the Spirit is the vehicle of love. All three persons are involved in creation, incarnation, and redemption.

So they are all involved with us now in our world, with you as you contemplate the icon. Each one bears a staff. Some say it is a royal sceptre; but others that it is a pilgrim's staff, a sign of God's constant effort to come to us and to the world he loves.

> Be adored among men,
> God, three-numbered form;...
> Beyond saying sweet, past telling of tongue
> Thou art lightning and love... (Hopkins)

## Is a Trinity really necessary?

The Israelites would die for the singleness of their God. To admit of more than one God was blasphemy. One overall God in heaven, rather than a race of quarrelling gods on Olympus. Why have three when One is enough? Don't make life more complicated than it need be.

Yet here we were, we Christians, inventing a Three-God. Not inventing, exactly, because it is there in the gospel, but we latched onto it, or Them. Who does one pray to, Father? or Jesus? or the Spirit? or just God? Why Three? I used to wonder.

At first I just took it on faith, imbibed with the milk. Jesus seemed to indicate two others apart from himself. He referred often and lovingly to his Father in heaven, in familiar terms and in such a way that you could not but feel it was essential to him. One way of summing up his whole purpose in life was to 'do the will of my Father'. The Spirit seemed to creep in by the back door, when Jesus left by the front. But if you look closely you will see that Spirit present through the gospel. Jesus pointed to the essential role that she would fulfil. So I had to accept that the Trinity was there to stay, whatever I thought about it. Yet the question remained, why three rather than one?

Again, what does it mean to say we are created in the image and likeness of God? The answer often given, that the likeness to God is our spiritual, intellectual side, seemed to me to lack something, only serving to emphasise the dualism that is always lurking in the wings of our faith.

The answer, in so far as there is one outside of mystery, is surely to be seen in the very nature of that God. God creates the way he is, Trinity.

The family at table in the Rublev icon seems so complete and self-contained. Nothing would seem to be able to disrupt the enclosed harmony of the scene. You feel you could never break into this circle. Here is the invulnerable, immovable, untouchable God once defined in the Fourth Lateran Council:

'We firmly believe and profess with sincere hearts that there is only One True Eternal, Incommensurable, Unchangeable, Incomprehensible, Omnipotent and Ineffable God.' Although every word of it is true I don't fancy trying to form a relationship with it, do you?

As you stare at the Rublev Trinity you might feel that you could never break into that circle. Yet the space in front of you is open, waiting for you, and there, behind their heads, are the emblems of creation, out there and beyond, yet part of the picture.

Three and One, One and Three. That is the paradoxical truth. Each looks to the other. The fact is, the very nature of God is to be in the other. Theologians coined a big word for it, Circumincession! (or, if you prefer Greek, Perichoresis!).

J.V. Taylor invented a beautiful term for it: 'In-othering'. Each person finds expression and being in and through the other. 'The Father and I are one', said Jesus.

Yet each one is a Person, an individual. The Father is not the Son, nor is the Son the Spirit, nor is the Spirit the Father. Each is a person in his or her own right. When God created, it was this being of his that was put there in creation, this Three-in-Oneness or rather, Being-in-the-Otherness. Our likeness to God is in our being like that ourselves. We are individuals with personality and individuality. Yet our being is expressed and realised in and through our relatedness to one another. It is not good for a man to be alone. Our very completion is in relationship. Yet we are distinct individuals, each one.

That relationship runs right through creation. The very act of creation was an ordering, a bringing together of what was chaos. God's love does this automatically, because that is the nature of God. He cannot but draw things together in his own being.

Creation is an act of love.
Creation is a never-ending outpouring of love,
An artwork ever striving to be born...

In the vision of Juliana of Norwich the whole of creation was a mere nut in the palm of Christ's hand, so tiny she wondered how it could survive. The answer came that it would survive because God loves it. She realised then that creation was an act of love. Love is God's nature, and is expressed in relationship. The image of God in us is not so much our spirituality or brains or will, but our potential for individuality to be expressed in relationship.

That relationship is not just to other human beings. The whole of creation is a ball of God's wool, a cosmos of God-relationships. We shall not understand our place on earth unless we face up to the way in which we are internally

16

related to the rest of the world. We have a special place, a special function in the world.

Stop and go out this evening after dark, and look at the sky and the stars.

> I kiss my hand
> To the stars, lovely asunder
> Starlight, wafting him out of it; and
> Glow, glory in thunder. (Hopkins)

This was a 'devotion' that St Ignatius loved. He would stare at the stars, because, he said, it made him want to serve God! Every night that sky is there. Think of its organization, its connectedness, its vastness. It makes you feel small!

> O God, your name rings gloriously around
>    the earth.
> Babies chant your praise.
> When I gaze up at those stars
> sprinkled over the heavens by your fingers
> and the sun and moon shaped by your hands
> I begin to wonder what we small humans are all about
>    and
> why you bother about us.
> But you have made us in your image,
> made us kings and queens of the earth
> to rule with you over all your creation, responsible
> for the sheep and cattle and rhinos and hippos
>    and elephants,
> lions, tigers, things in the sky, things in the sea,
> the lot! What a responsibility!
> Too much, unless we remember to praise
> Your Name, Loving Creator of the Universe.
>
> (Psalm 8)

Go out in the daytime and look at some small part of nature, a detail such as a leaf or piece of bark. Notice again the care, the necessary mechanisms that went to its making, the systems that must have cooperated to produce it.

Oh my! How I want to bless you, Great Creator!
Up there in a ball of light! Aglow with majesty and
glory! (Psalm 104)

Just as we need to take up a stance with respect to the world and creation I think we have to take a stance to God. As before, it does not mean that we deny other parts of reality, but simply find that certain aspects of the truth are more helpful to us than others. Different saints have embodied different ways of coming to God. Different composers stress different aspects of the global reality of music. Because Giuseppe Verdi composed mostly operas it does not invalidate the symphonies of Sibelius. So we have to make choices in our ways of finding where life is centred for us.

We have to choose what sort of God we worship. As I have already partly indicated there are two very different Gods up there in heaven. There is the God of Lateran IV Council, who is untouchable, static and abstract, at least in our definitions, whose very being is to exist. He is described as 'pure act', a necessary being, that is, one who could not NOT exist! Another word used of him is 'impassable', that is, incapable of suffering or being roused or touched. He knows everything by knowing himself. He exists 'a se' as the Latin tag has it, that is, he has no need of anything or anyone outside of himself. His 'infinite perfection', signifies that he cannot be influenced by any being outside of himself. So, strictly speaking, he cannot be in relationship with anything apart from himself! That would change him. Theologians used to say that while we are in relationship to God he cannot be in relationship to us! Any relationship between a creature and God is real only on the part of the creature.

All of this sounds rather like theological hard chew, I know, but it was the God I was brought up with and could not relate to until I realised that there was another side to God. It is all perfectly true, of course, it is consistent with a way of seeing God, it is magnificent in describing God's transcendence, his separateness from his creation, apartheid, holiness.

But when God created something other than himself and gave it autonomy he put an end to any idea of a quiet life wrapped in a cloud of his own perfection. He then took on the aspect of God which we call Immanent, the one who is with us. It is Immanuel of the bible, God-with-us. This is the one who is found in the very fabric of creation, in and through it. He is, of course, much more than creation, but is to be found there, not merely confronting it as a Transcendent being, but present right in it. The community of all living things, in communion with God and each other, is formed by the Spirit acting throughout creation. Yet each individual thing acts in its own way.

Nothing in our world stands isolated and totally independent of everything else. The being of every single thing is as a part of a network of being, so that it exists by, with or from other things, in and for others. When we think of the nature of God, as Three in One, One in Three, this is not surprising. God created in his image (how else could he create?) and so we will find his nature reflected in ours, in the conjunction of our separateness from each other as discrete individuals and at the same time a connectedness with everything else. We used to search for the image of God by seeing threeness in things but that is surely not necessary. Rather should we not be surprised to find the dynamic tension of the individual having a being distinct from the rest yet in relationship of dependence and co-existence with the rest. In oneself, and in the other.

We are part of a many-sided, intricate network of relationships, person to person, people to people, and each one to God, of person to the earth.

It has been pointed out (by Moltmann) that we have used words like 'making', 'preserving', 'maintaining', 'perfecting' but that these words express a God-creator remote from his work. So we need to add words like 'indwelling', 'sympathising', 'participating', 'accompanying', 'enduring', 'delighting', and 'glorifying'.

I talk of two Gods, but in fact there is only one. God is so great as to compass both of these realities, Transcendence and Immanence, even though to us they seem contradictory.

It will make a great difference how we pray which God we think we are praying to. Try to pray the incident of the 'Burning Bush', in Exodus 3:1-6. It describes an experience of Moses in which he sensed the presence of the Otherness of God, the Transcendent God. Or go with Elijah to Horeb in 1 Kings 19:1-18 and be with him in the presence of that Transcendent God in the still small voice of the wind. That sense of God's otherness fills the human being with awe so that his flesh tingles.

We do well to reflect on God's creating act. We can do this by finding a quiet place and reading aloud to ourselves the opening chapters of the Book of Genesis. Don't read it as a scientific thesis but as a hymn or chant. Try to sense God's exuberance in the act of creation.

God's revelation: first of all, in time came his revelation in creation itself. Before ever a bible was thought of, before gospels and even the arrival of the Word Himself in time, for aeons and aeons God's glory shone out in creation. Indeed, until the arrival of humankind creation had no voice except its own value and splendour, indeed veritatis splendor! Then God was revealed in a particular way through the chosen people, and then in the fullest way in his son. God laboured (and still does!) to provide, to give, to declare.

We are called by God into being and throughout our lives. He calls us to himself; but he calls us as He has made us, created beings in a material creation. The temptation is to think that holiness consists in denying our createdness, to spiritualise ourselves into angels. That is not the way God made us, and not the way we give him glory. We come to him in and through our createdness, not aside from it. We give glory to him in our bodies as well as our souls and minds. To deny the body is tantamount to telling God that he created rubbish, something unclean. This is not to say that appetite must be given free reign. Yet it must also not be suppressed. This is no news to any of us, yet we have consistently imaged the spiritual life in these terms. God moves towards embodiment. Creation receives its full meaning in the Incarnation, enfleshment of God.

Created as I am I must use things. Discernment is needed to decide which things lead me to God, which away.

Creation is a never-ending outpouring of love
An artwork ever striving to be born...
And on the seventh day God rested from his labours,
So worn, so emptied by his restless working
And tense and anxious like a mother
yearning to hear the loving response of her children...

God had to wait. Anyone who loves has to wait for a response and in the waiting they are restless and open to disappointment. God had to wait for the response of his creation, for in making something other than oneself, however much that thing is part of oneself, one makes oneself vulnerable and open to disappointment. Because the response may not come, or if it does it may well be negative. Love is involved and that means it can never be selfish. Parents create out of love, yet once the child is there they have to relate to him or her, that is to another person, different from themselves.

When you love someone that beloved person assumes power over you, power to hurt, greater in proportion as the love is greater. When you love someone you become open to that person and all protection of the heart is dispensed with.

For God's love to be fulfilled it needs the responding cry from creation. The history related in the bible is often relating how that response was not given.

Why did I find no one when I came?
Why did no one answer when I called? (Is 50)

Love that is not responded to is still waiting in the wings. Since God is Love it is not surprising that there is a whole literature about God as vulnerable and labouring.

God in his love for me is constantly at work,
Like a potter moulding into the clay
the inspiration of his spirit,
He labours as a mother labours in giving birth
in order to share his life and his love.
He is at work ceaselessly in the cosmos,
weaving a tapestry of stars, and galaxies,
forming all the elements, the trees and shrubs,
grasses and microbes, heavy beasts and things that go
zing in the night ... every one gives such glory to Him
because he gives them being, life, sensation and
keeps them living, feeling, reproducing.
                    (Contemplatio ad amorem of St Ignatius)

I remember the surprise I felt when first encountering the idea of God working and labouring for me, and for creation. It had always been a matter of my working to be better, to be forgiven, to become a truer child of God. To find, suddenly, that the effort is all the other way, that it is God who has to make the effort seemed to take the initia-

22

tive away from me altogether. At first this was undermining since it left me with nothing to do about my salvation; then it came as a relief to know that God is and always will be at work for the good of the earth and all creation. It reminds us that God is the originator, the beginning and source.

It is comforting to know that the doctrine that you can work for your own salvation is in fact an old heresy, once propounded by a worthy British monk called Pelagius, a thoroughly good man who did much good work and said many good things, but in this particular overstretched orthodoxy. We can, according to Pelagius, pull ourselves up by our own bootstrings.

Again I remember the sense of shock on reading that Meister Eckhardt, the mystic, in answer to the question, 'What does God DO all day?' replied, 'She lies on a bed giving birth!' I had got used to the idea of God as mother, and I think I could cope with the thought of her giving birth to a child called creation, but the idea of her being permanently on the bed of labour seemed a bit too much. Yet it emphasises the degree to which God is at work constantly in creation, not just once upon a time, but now and always, giving birth.

The best way of thinking of God's relationship to the creation is perhaps that of the parent to the child. It is a constantly changing relationship, growing and deepening and involving tension and growing pains. So it must be between God and us. Our relationship is not static, and if it is found to be so we are probably refusing growth.

It is difficult for us to come to terms with the freedom of creation. We have been given a great autonomy and we don't know how to use it. We seem to go in two directions at once, wanting God to intervene ('why does He allow this to happen?') and at the same time wanting Him to leave us alone. We are like children in that respect, wanting to be 'free' of parental control, wanting to stay out at night and play in any way that we want, yet only too glad to run back to them when the going gets beyond our control. Perhaps a reason for God's annoying silence in prayer is precisely this: he is asking us to stand on our own feet and not be running back to the parental apron strings whenever things go wrong, when we are so willing to dispense with his care when things go right!

Alongside of this frightening autonomy is the recognition that we cannot stand on our own. We are totally dependent on God! So we spend much time in our lives, 'seeking the will of God.' But what is this 'Will of God?' Is God an Absolute Controller who regulates and controls every event, minor or major, in the working of the universe? Such that no one can think, move, be, unless it is written in the blueprint of God's will? This way of thinking leads to a stultifying dependence. We become the servants who wait upon the Lord, watching for the movement of his hand before we act. As a retreat director I have witnessed people searching, year in, year out, for the 'will of God', some clear sign or indication of 'his will'. They are asking for a glimpse of that blueprint so as to see what to do next. And God seems to keep the blueprint tantalisingly hidden behind his back. The result is a constant unfulfilled search, with the consequent feeling that what I am doing is NOT the will of God, but my own inclination and need.

There is a deep mystery here, because in some sense it is true that God is the controller. Yet the very nature of creation is such that autonomy is built into it by the act of making something other than God's self. When parents create a child they wish, no doubt, to create something in their own image, a person who will perpetuate their being. At the same time they know very well that once created that child becomes person in their own right, and may well move apart, physically, mentally and spiritually, from themselves, and their duty in love is to allow that to happen and even encourage it.

24

Therein lies the agony. The love lavished on the child may not be responded to, may even be blamed for curbing the freedom of the child. God wishes us to love him, but to do so freely, of our own will. He will not coerce our love.

*Here are some texts that you may want to pray on, apart from those given in the text:*

Isaiah 55:1-3: Come to the water
Micah 4:10: Pains of labour
Isaiah 13:8 and 42:14: A woman in labour
John 16:21-22: A woman in childbirth suffers
Isaiah 49:14,15: I will never forget you

# CHAPTER 2

# 'I to I'

## My relationship to myself

Imagine the Sower going out to sow the seed. Mark 4:1-9.
I stand and watch. The seed flies through the air and lands
in different places. Some of it is on the path where the birds
are quick to gobble it up. Some of it lands on rocky ground
where the soil is thin, giving scanty root-room, so it sprouts
quickly and as quickly is scorched to death by the sun. I see
some of the seed dropping among the brambles which
choke it. But there is seed that falls into good soil and
grows up fruitfully in varying degrees.

Imagine now that the whole area, path, rocks, brambles,
good soil is yourself. You are the field. St Paul tells us that
we are God's field for the ploughing. The seed, then, is
God's life and word coming to you. Part of you receives it,
other parts refuse it; or again, there are times when you are
more receptive to the word, other times less so.

The theme of this book is that God's being, his Threeness
and Oneness is expressed in the whole of creation. Creation is like a mushroom culture, an interweaving of strands
and connections. There has been much written in recent
years about the connectedness of creation. God's Threeness,
the interrelationship between the Persons, is represented in
creation by this interweaving of the threads of the cosmos.

Yet God's Oneness must also be there. Each Person of
the Trinity is an Individual, a separate being whose individuality is paradoxically expressed in the other. I am
created in his image so in my being I will reflect both that
oneness and that relationship to the other.

I live in a world which consists of relationships, and it is in and through these that I express what God made me to be. I am in relationship, first of all, to God who made me, and particularly with Jesus Christ. I am in relationship to others about me, to all the people of the world. I have a particular relationship to the world in which I live, to the earth.

But there is another relationship that I can be said to form, and that is within myself. This may sound strange, being related to oneself. Yet it is recognised within our ordinary speech when we say things like, 'He is at odds with himself', or 'She is a divided person', or 'Pull yourself together'. Kierkegaard once described the self as 'a relation that relates itself to its own self'.

One day your inner spirits are high, a large cheque, whether monetary or cultural, has just been paid into your account, your project has been praised, your team has won, or the boss has smiled at your work product (chances of promotion?) or your girlfriend or boyfriend has smiled at you... everything in the landscape is bathed in sunlight, and God is in his heaven and the angels are preening their wings. The following week your friend calls you a selfish ****, or prefers someone else, your team is hanged, lost and quartered, the boss tips your work into the bin, you run at a steep angle into a depression, God falls out of heaven (was he really there in the first place?), the angels fall off their perches and your faith plummets with them.

Are we not tempted to say, in the good times, that our faith, our prayer, will stand firm no matter what else should collapse? 'Though all should desert you I will not!' said Peter, shortly before he denied the Lord and ran off with the others. The building seems so firm before the earthquake comes. When the catastrophe arrives the whole structure comes crashing down, faith, hope and charity. We are not homogeneous beings. Our field consists of different and unequal parts. Maybe we are musical, and we are

28

stirred to our depths when we hear Verdi's Requiem. Through the very music our religious roots dig deeper into the ground of our being and into God. But then we read some book that tells us that music is only a feeling and has nothing to do with real religious conviction, and our roots wither and die and the whole tree falls over.

Look inside this field of yours and see what a contradictory mixture it is! Lent comes, and your sacrificial spirit wants to go to great lengths of self-denial. Two days later, at the Jones's, the box of chocolates goes round, your eyes widen, your pupils dilate, and your hand slips into the box in advance of the memory of your resolution. You are happily married, you love your husband, yet you find yourself flirting outrageously with his best friend down at the pub. You wish to be slim and attractive, but your desire for food makes the chances of it even slimmer. You may be a priest who loves the ministry, yet you desperately want to have a family. You want to be free and confined, living a simple life, but with every luxury. You want to have your cake and eat it. This is the field on which the Sower comes to sow the seed. Not that these sentiments succeed each other in the field, like the seasons. No, they are all there at the same time!

I imagine my field, then, in order to detect the state of my soil, where my rocks are, and where my brambles, which parts of me are receptive, and which are not, when are the times when the word is able to take root, and when does it not even get a look in?

The need to take a stance in my life will consist in the discernment of times or circumstances when the word is refused entry or is smothered out of existence; and my action will be to avoid such times or at least to be forewarned against them. At the same time I am well aware that what is most negative in me may be the very thing God uses for his purposes.

Psychology speaks to religion today in words of wisdom. We are not, after all, disembodied souls, but whole people, or we aspire to be. Or do we?

Do we? I ask the question as I look at the calendar of saints and wonder whether holiness and wholeness go together. May I be wrong, but I am not struck by the 'wholeness' of some of the saints. Some, I know, achieved a wonderful integrity, but for many austerity that bordered on eccentricity was reckoned the primary virtue. Indeed, that seems to be the very thing that some of them were canonised for! Who could call Simon Stylites a 'balanced' character, apart from his doubtful achievement of balancing on a pillar? It does not seem that being a whole person, in the modern sense of being psychologically integrated, really counted as a factor in holiness. Heaven, it seems, is peopled with citizens who flew over the cuckoo's nest.

Furthermore, it often appears that what counts for holiness is an excess of asceticism, a killing of the bodily powers as a means of promoting the power of the spirit.

Perhaps we need to look at the gospel. I do not get the impression that that was the spirit of Jesus. He was a man of remarkable power, but that power was used to express the compassion and care of the Father in heaven. Christ gave every appearance of wishing human beings to be whole, not diseased or crippled by bugs or by sin. He did want whole people, because that was the way God had created and creation is to give glory to God, not to pronounce it a botch! Many of the most glorious passages in the gospels reveal a Christ preoccupied with restoring wholeness to that which was diseased or distorted out of its true nature. Human beings are not disembodied souls.

Yet the emphasis in spirituality has often been on the saving of souls alone, as though that were God's only interest. In which case, why did he create embodied people?

God creates me, knits me together in the womb of my

mother. He creates out of love, so his creating me is an act of love. And just as he looked on creation, and saw that it was good, so does he look on me and see that I am good. With Mary, therefore, I can say the Magnificat and apply it to myself.

If I am to grow spiritually I need greater self-awareness, and then self-acceptance which is not the same thing. Eventually, with God's help, I may achieve a measure of self-transcendence. Self-awareness is simply the ability to be aware of what is going on within myself, my feelings, my reactions, attitudes, what my motivation is when I act.

Such introspection may seem, almost by definition, self-centred. Self-centredness often sounds selfish. Some authors take the view that we are beings of relationship and that the separate self is just an illusion. They have accepted the 'in-othering' aspect of God in us, but refused to acknowledge that the Persons in God are individuals, each different from the other. William Johnston wrote: 'This notion of a separate self or ego is an illusion...' I think this is but half the truth. There is a self and I need to be aware of it. Its nature is to be in relation to God and other selves. Yet if there is no self there is nothing to be in relationship.

It is as well to recall that a lot will depend on the way I look at God. If I am convinced that God is immanent, present in his creation, and that his spirit is within me (I am a temple of the Holy Spirit said the penny catechism) then when I look into the deeps of my own self I am also finding the Spirit at work, drawing me to a more Christlike life.

What is often called 'Faith History' is a way of looking back over my life to appreciate what God has done for me. It would be a pity if this were restricted to 'churchy' things, such as baptism, confirmation, learning my prayers, and so on. God's action takes place all through my life, in every department, not just in the churchy bits. The image of God in me permeates my whole life. If we see God as interested,

31

not just in my soul, but in the whole of me, then the Faith History must be an introspection into the whole of my life to discover in what I have grown and in what I have been prevented from growing.

God has created me to be a unique individual, a being that has never been, nor will ever be, quite duplicated or replicated. If God has a plan for me, it must be that I will fulfil the potential of this unique individual, this me. My uniqueness is often referred to nowadays, in a phrase coined by Fr Herbert Alfonso SJ, as 'Personal Vocation'. Again, let us avoid the trap of making my vocation an exclusively 'religious' or churchy thing. Each person is called to a particular way of being which is, for that person, a special vocation, their own path to God. A certain Rabbi Zusya, shortly before he died, is recorded as saying: When I go to Judgment I will not be asked, 'Why were you not Moses, but why were you not Zusya?' The same goes for us. At the judgment we will not be asked, Why were you not St Francis de Sales, or St Ignatius, but why were you not Tom or Sheila, the person I wanted you to be?

Try looking at your life as a dart-board with the different layers of commitment and responsibility as you work in from the outside of the board. Not that you deliberately choose the various layers of your life, but nevertheless, once born into them you choose an attitude or stance towards them.

First and foremost, you are called to be human. It is so basic a part of our calling as to be overlooked. The stubbing out of our humanity has been a deliberate part of the training of many religious. Yet it is a fundamental commitment. God has often been used as an excuse for avoiding it.

We are then further called to be a member of a family, this or that particular family and to express our love of God in and through it. We are committed to a particular religious persuasion perhaps, to a school as a student. Marriage brings its own new commitments and responsibilities which supercede but do not abolish the other ones. Or we may find ourselves called to a religious rule with its own inspiration and colour.

These can all be seen like concentric circles on the dartboard; and there at the centre is the bullseye, my own self.

> Each mortal thing does one thing and the same...
> Selves – goes itself; myself it speaks and spells,
> Crying, what I do is me; for that I came. (Hopkins)

Sitting with retreatants I am often struck by the frequency of bad self-image, the person who cannot see any good in themselves or believe in themselves as beings who are loved by God. Engaged in a never-ending search for the right way, the path to God, their vocation, they fail to see the map that is written into their very being. It is everyone's vocation to unfold the unique being that they are, and bring it to God developed and fruitful. Instead, so much energy and prayer is expended on searching for ways that will manufacture an image of St Ignatius or St Francis or Rabbi So&So or Guru Howdoyoudo. These saints and teachers may have a great deal to teach us, but finally our path must be our own. It is a far greater challenge to find that within ourselves, than to open someone else's map and try to follow in their footsteps.

I need to search for, and listen to, the calling. It will involve my particular gifts and inclinations. It will involve, in other words, discernment. Spend time looking at the Potter in Jeremiah 18. Do what the prophet Jeremiah was told to do: go down to the Potter's shed and watch him at work. It is a creation image. God created man out of the dust of the earth. On the doorway of Chartres cathedral there is a series of carvings and one of them is the creation of Adam. God sits with Adam beside him, the creature's head resting in the Creator's lap, and God is moulding him into shape. We sing 'You are the potter, we are the clay!' In other words, God is creating me now. So I watch Him at work, creating me, moulding me. Am I happy with what I see or dissatisfied?

Faith History is a prayerful remembering of my past in order to see more clearly how I, this individual, has been encouraged to grow, and how it has been prevented from doing so.

If this Faith History is done like homework it will become bogged down and blighted! Don't try to be too chronological or even logical, but let come up whatever wants to surface. Allow yourself to remember things from childhood that seem to have lodged in your memory. They have probably stuck there for some reason. Allow yourself the freedom to dwell on places, scenes, atmosphere, that enabled you to expand. Remember people who were influential to you, and books you read that went deep, or events that expressed something in you that was good.

On the other hand, flotsam and jetsam from childhood may rise to the surface that you would rather forget, which cause pain, like the articles of clothing that rise up from a submarine that has been hit by a depth-charge! It may be that the Faith History is a means of the healing of memories, those festering wounds that we have never had occasion to bandage or address. They need to be addressed, because, as Cardinal Hume says in his book, they 'enslave and sadden us and make us limp and less effectual for God's work'.

Crises, like bereavement or divorce, can become the watersheds that lead into self-awareness. The emotional disturbance caused seems to provide the stimulus for a time of deep but painful enlightenment. In a striking image the poet Adrienne Rich speaks of this in the poem 'Diving into the Wreck', an exploration into the self, which no amount of reading or advice can replace. The theories of Jung and

34

Freud may help and guide but finally each one has to discover for him or herself. It is a dangerous search in depths which are unknown to us.

'Oh the mind, mind has mountains, cliffs of fall...
   ...no-man fathomed,'

as Manley Hopkins puts it.

Progress into the depths of this inner journey is slow and filled with question and doubt. I seem to get nowhere; then progress becomes awkward and painful. I don't know what I am meeting, whether 'this is it' or not, whether I am running into danger. These waters never seem to be like the description in the book... There is a feeling of 'blacking out', not being able to cope. The wreck shows me the damage that was done, the weaknesses, the catastrophes. But hidden in the hold I find treasures to be brought to the surface and built upon.

Self awareness involves looking at the negative parts of myself as well as the positive.

Self-acceptance goes further, to the willingness to accept the way I am, to accept the temperament God has given me, to grow where I am planted. It may even encompass my own sinfulness and the knowledge that things are not and will not be perfect or the way I want them to be. There seems to be a paradox in this. How can I 'accept' my own sinfulness? Surely I am called to fight against it, strive to become perfect? How can my relationship to Christ and to others be right as long as I am a sinner? Yet the story of the sinners in the gospel, the Prodigal Son especially, shows us a God who requires us to recognise our sinfulness and joyfully accept forgiveness. We are asked to accept that we are accepted despite being sinners. It is precisely the ones who think they are sinless that Jesus harangues. Even in our human relationships the person who is righteous is often more of a problem that an honest-to-God sinner!

Jung sets great importance on self-acceptance. Our Christian upbringing has taught us to love our enemies, forgive insults and turn the other cheek, until we find that the enemy is within us, whereupon condemnation and denial take the place of forgiveness.

Self-transcendence is perhaps particularly the area of extra help from God, to enable us to go beyond what seems to be the limit, to grow, to love. This may involve risk and the leaving of old securities in life. It is simpler not to move, to stay with what I find easy and familiar. As Dylan Thomas remarks in his poem *Was there a time* safety lies in ignorance and the only way to keep your hands clean is to have no arms!

Discernment is required to see in what I am asked to move. Jesus invited the apostles to move out into the deep water. I listen to the movements within me, being aware of my own feelings and reactions. The Spirit, working within me, draws in a particular way, through my desires, inclinations, aspirations. When the Spirit draws and I respond in faith I will feel consolation. When I feel disturbance it can mean it is not a true drawing, or it can mean that there is resistance within me.

My image of God is inevitably involved. A good image will reinforce the drawing of the Spirit, but a bad one will pull against it, thus causing desolation. A demanding God who never smiles may be causing me to 'mortify' myself, when the Spirit is in fact calling for more love. Conflict and desolation ensue.

In the famous chapter 13 of 1 Corinthians, the chapter on love, there is a passage about maturing.

When I was a child I used to speak like a child and think like a child, and reason like a child; but now I am an adult these childish ways have been put aside.

I can ask myself, have these childish ways been put aside? As often as not, like the field we started the chapter with, we are not homogeneous. Some of our reactions are still those of a child, and have not matured in the spirit. Let us meditate and pray that our individual selves may grow into the full image of God in us.

*Passages that may help you to pray:*

Ephesians 3:14-16: May your inner self grow strong
1 Corinthians 13:11&12: Childish ways left behind
Luke 6:39-45: The plank in my eye
Luke 13:18-21: The yeast and the mustard seed
Mark 4:1-9: The Sower cast the seed

# CHAPTER 3

# 'Eye to Eye'

## Relating to the other

Love 'creates' neighbour. The object of my charity cannot be defined by law.

Place yourself, in your imagination, at a vantage point from which you can witness, or enter into, the scene described by Jesus which we know as The Good Samaritan (Luke 10:29-37).

To us the question of the lawyer to Jesus, 'Who is my neighbour?' may seem naive. We think we know who our neighbour is. But for that Jewish lawyer it was not an idle question. Their law and customs forbade commerce with outsiders. To assist a Gentile woman in childbirth would be to help bring a Gentile into the world and so was wrong. 'Neighbour' for the Jew meant relatives or friends, or at least fellow Jews. Not the foreigner. So, for Jesus to present the neighbour as a Samaritan, one who was traditionally not just outside the pale, but hostile, amounted to confrontation with the Jewish attitude of the time.

The Samaritan it was who went away justified because he had created the neighbour by his love. He did not wait for the law to tell him whom to love. Human need demanded it of him and he gave freely.

Neighbour defines the parameters of our relationships to our fellow human beings. There is a line of poetry that expresses for me with the incisiveness of a laser, the nature of our being in relationship:

I am through you so I. (E.E. Cummings)

In this short line are expressed both the uniqueness of the individual person, and yet the person that can only be expressed and fulfilled in and through the other.

You will know that I am in my Father,
and you in me,
just as I am in you (John 14:20).

Creation is permeated with the relationships of the Trinity. The same love that gives being to the Father, Son and Spirit is that which is in Jesus, and in and through every human being. The image of God in us is the tension of individuality expressed in and through neighbour. Our nature is to be in relationship to others, to God, to creation.

If anyone love me he will keep my word
and my Father will love him (John 14).

Sin came in to twist and break these ties and hence the need for us to be constantly reminded that love is of our essence.

Relationships are the glory and the curse of human living. Relationship, that is, to other people. Individual unique person I may be but I am also an atom within a molecule, distinguishable as a separate entity, yet having no separate existence. My atom is always in combination with other atoms. We are each created with a 'valency' (another term from the chemistry book!), the combining power of an atom. Our instinct and nature is to be 'combined' with other atoms to form various types of molecule. 'No man is an island entire of itself; every man is a piece of the continent...'

'It is not good for the man to be alone,' God declared at creation, 'I will make him a consort like himself.' And the man and woman became one flesh... and God saw that it was good.

Some time ago a naturalist, Jane Goodall, spent years in the jungle observing the habits of chimpanzees. In describing their social mores she remarked that 'one chimpanzee is no chimpanzee!' Communal by nature as they are, their being is not expressed in solitude. So too the human is naturally in relation and fullness is lost in isolation.

I cannot be me, be myself, be truly human, except through you. The film cliche, 'we were made for each other' is literally true. The fall was precisely a disastrous breach in communion, at all levels of relationship. The person became disconnected from God, from the earth, within the self, and from the other.

Even the saddest cases of the breakdown of human relationships, the marriages that disintegrate, the people searching again and again for companionship, even these negative experiences highlight our human inbuilt 'valency'.

How wrong to suggest that you can only be yourself by freeing yourself from the shackles of companionship and the commerce of society, by suppressing the other rather than being set free by him or her. If I think I have nothing to receive I am denying something central to my humanity and theirs.

God the Father could not be God without the Son, in fact could not be Father without Son. Relationship cannot be thought of as an 'added extra' tacked on to make us feel good, any more than being my parents' child is incidental. A single note in a tune or symphony cannot stand alone. We are the single note, enmeshed in a complicated texture of creation-music.

God-Persons mutually constitute each other, as do we – we make each other what we are. The deepest bond that expresses this in our world is the unity in one flesh of man and wife, the bond in each other's very being. Our individuality in community is the fruit of being bound up with each other (for better or for worse!) in the bundle of life.

We are but a pale shadow of God's being, of course, as

41

we struggle through space and time. But that pale shadow is the silver lining that gilds our being-in-relationship with the whole universe, with its massive history stretching away back before ever there were human cultures and traditions.

The sense of total connectedness of creation, of our own dependence on God, on one another, on the material world itself is being stressed by feminist theologians today. The feminine is more open to finding God in personal connections, than in abstract reason, in tracing the in-other nature of God in our own connection with the other in our lives. The woman's instinct is to bring into embrace rather than separate out and in this way more truly represents the unifying nature of God. She looks for the possibilities of personal interaction and growth, the drawing out of potential, and drawing things into unity.

R.S. Thomas in the poem *The Way of It* speaks of the woman 'at work always, mending the garment of our marriage' and, after an altercation, 'busy after for hours, rubbing smiles into the wounds'. She sees and acts intuitively, aware of roots and branches simultaneously, the beginnings of things and their creative value, the conception of new life and possibility.

Though we are individuals, and ignore the fact at our peril, our nature is to be in relationship. We depend on others, on God, on the material world for our very existence. In the Spiritual Exercises St Ignatius expects us to exclaim with surprise that when we recognise our sinfulness we also realise that nevertheless the universe continues to support us! We depend on others. Isolation is hell. We can, as C.S. Lewis wrote in *Four Loves*, seal ourselves into a tomb where we become preserved in stone, our hearts no longer breakable. Yet it is necessary for us to be individuals in our relating to each other. An empty shell relates emptily.

We learned the Ten Commandments at school as edicts

from above. They seemed so peremptory; yet they are based on the nature of the human being, which is based in turn on the nature of God. By telling us not to desecrate creation they aim to remind us of the need to respect each other and God and creation. Respect is the key word. We are to respect others as selves who have as much right as we ourselves have. Respect is an aspect of love.

In her book on the Ten Commandments, *Smoke on the Mountain* Joy Davidman related the story of the couple who lived in a house with their young son and one of the grandfathers. Grandad got old and doddery and began to be messy in his eating and general deportment. In disgust the couple consigned him to the corner, made him eat out of a bowl with a spoon, and eventually gave him a trough to eat his food from. One day, seeing their young son whittling some wood they asked him what he was doing. 'I'm making a trough for you and daddy to eat out of when you are old!'

Injustice and oppression hit the headlines today, in their flagrant violation of human rights and hence their total disregard for the inherent dignity of the human being. In this they constitute a violation of right relationship, ruptured by sin. 'Do unto others what you would have them do to you.' Where there is injustice and oppression respect has disappeared and relationship has been twisted and displaced by domination. A man says to his neighbour in effect, 'you are no longer my neighbour but my servant. I am your master.'

The fox in *The Little Prince* feels unable to play with the Little Prince precisely because he is not 'tamed', and describes taming as the forging of ties or relationships between people.

The annals of romantic fiction are full of the taming of the wildest natures by loving relationship, aggression giving way to gentleness. Even in the world of wolves where the aggressive instinct is proverbial, the natural savagery is thwarted by a gesture of turning the neck to the other, exposing a vulnerable part.

Close relationship is by its nature helpful and graced. When I am involved deeply with another, the sense of trust that is engendered enables me to be totally open about myself, and to reveal both strength and weakness. Being able to speak about my woundedness, turning my vulnerability to my partner, dissipates any aggression and allows for healing to take place. When I trust that the relationship is lasting and that healing takes places I find growth and maturing. Yet growth is painful, because of our sinful nature. It demands a gradual forfeit of our defensive pride and attempts to shore up our inadequacy by aggression. As the Horse explained to the Velveteen Rabbit becoming 'real' (or myself, or meaningful, or human, or related) involves having your fur rubbed off.

Ursula Le Guin's *Earthsea Trilogy* uses a biblical term to indicate a more-than-casual relationship, 'Naming'. Each person has a name by which he is known to all, but also an inner name which is known to very few, those with whom he is truly intimate, especially God. Try the exercise of drawing a dartboard, write in the outside circle those who know you most superficially, and as you go in towards centre the layers of intimacy, until at the bulls-eye those only who know you most intimately. Does anyone really KNOW you? Perhaps only God does.

How does God estimate our Christian life on earth? How does he judge it? Place yourself in imagination in a great Hall of Judgement. See masses of people crowding in, and at the front, looking down, the great Judge, Christ. What is he saying as he separates one group from another? Is it, 'You have kept the Lenten Fast, you have been a regular Mass-goer or you have said your prayers?' No. He is saying, 'I was hungry and you fed me, thirsty and you gave me a drink, as a stranger you welcomed me, you clothed my nakedness, you visited me in sickness, came to me when I was in prison. Come, you blessed' Mt 25:31-46.

It is so simple, so human, we do not think of it as Christlike. 'Anybody can do that, you don't have to be a Christian.' Quite right. So Christ wants us to be wholly human. Anybody is saved by Christ who does these things.

I do not for a moment want to suggest that going to Mass and saying one's prayers are not important. I simply say they do not seem to be the criteria by which we are judged, according to St Matthew's gospel. That is the way our image of God is lived out in our lives, that is the way our love (and God is love) is expressed.

Our prayer and Mass and devotions are important. They are a direct expression to God of praise and need. Any relationship will consist of a pattern of different levels. A married man will go to the building site, or office, in the morning. He may go for a drink with his friends in the pub, go to the football, come home and have a meal with the family, play with the children. But then there will be times when he will be close to his wife, in conversation or making love. All of these activities are part of his married life. Yet the times of intimacy are core experiences that cannot be missed out. Prayer is the time of intimacy in the relationship to Christ, a personal and close meeting.

The primacy of relationship in our world and the need to reconstitute relationship which has been broken makes forgiveness a central theme of the gospel. In our imperfect existence, in our sinfulness, the bonds that unite us all in the Trinity are broken. Forgiveness is that act of recreation which mends them, or better, recreates them.

If we are unforgiving we are not fit for the kingdom, or for the offering of the altar since we are told to go and be reconciled before offering our gift. We are asked to forgive as we are forgiven. Peter is told that forgiveness is not limited, but, like God's, is unlimited.

Forgiveness is of the will. Whatever my feelings are

saying, whatever hurt and injustice there may have been, I will the good of the other, I refuse to wish harm to them. This entails sacrificing my own need for justice or revenge, and is a sort of death.

One aspect of our relationships highlights the deep strands of connection with those outside us that exist in us, often undetected. It is that aspect which Carl Jung points to as 'the shadow'. The Shadow refers to that part of us which we have suppressed and pushed under, in the interests of those ideals and structures built up in our childhood and youth. It is the furniture we do not like and so we put it down in the cellar and try to forget it is there. Or the slave we keep locked up in the basement.

How do we know the slave is there? We become aware of him in others, we project our shadow out onto the person we do not like. Ask someone to give a description of the personality traits they find impossible to get on with in somebody else, and they will describe their own shadow! When we find someone who really gets under our skin, and we find ourselves reacting to her or him in a totally irrational way we are looking at our own shadow. Others can see it, we cannot. These very qualities are so unacceptable to us precisely because they are our own repressed side. Only what we find unacceptable in ourselves do we find impossible to live with in others. This stranger, the shadow, must be recognised within ourselves. It is not easy to do so, but it is the door into ourselves and our reactions to others.

What can we do about this dark thing once we have recognised it? We can repress it but that is dangerous, we can try to fight it by will power, but that is wrong. All we can do is to 'suffer' it, as part of our personality. If not, we isolate ourselves from reality and begin to blame outside circumstances: 'If only this had happened!' or 'If only SHE had not been here!' By taking on this attitude we often CAUSE the very effect we are blaming. Recognising it involves suffering it as part of ourselves.

46

In your prayer remain with the scripture suggested in the text. Reflect on the relationships you have had through your life. How do you find yourself in relationship? Are you dominating, subservient, always trying to be helpful (the compulsive Helper?), do you receive more than you give?

As Christians our person-to-person relationships must include a relationship to God in Christ. Because Jesus is not tangibly present it is in danger of becoming an I-It rather than an I-Thou, that turns our faith will into religion. So we need to make sure that our life of faith and prayer is not thinking ABOUT Christ but meeting him. This was the preoccupation of the early church and especially Paul, not so much to 'say' things about Xt but to meet him as he himself had done on the road to Damascus. The apostles and disciples of Jesus knew only too well that their faith stemmed from personal encounter rather than from reading books or tracts or even hearing things said, though that may well be where it starts from. Praying in the gospels, then, becomes a meeting place. Go into your inner room and meet him there.

The strength of our Christian commitment must be rooted in a relationship with Christ. It will have developed and grown over the years; it may well not be the same as it was. The 'gentle Jesus meek and mild' of childhood may have given way to a more adult Christ. Or initial enthusiasm of conversion may have ceased to bubble and become more pedestrian.

Part of our humanness is to be in relationship. If Jesus was really human he must not only have been in relationship, but needed it. It is a two-way thing, dialogue not monologue.

His prime relationship was with his father in heaven. This seemed to be the essence of the man. If we were to point to one aspect of Jesus that would constitute his 'personal vocation' it would surely be his relationship to his

47

Father. That is what made him tick, that is where his energy and life came from. It is his 'divinity'. But a relationship 'grows' and develops. Can we say that this happened to Jesus? He was incarnated as Son of God, but he also grew more into it, adapted to it, responded to it. Jesus is 'Firstborn'. This implies two things, Sonship and Brotherhood. Son of the Father, Brother of all humankind. Brotherhood is part of his humanity. We know Jesus the Son only in brotherly/sisterly communion with him in the following his path of faith. He is the Way, Truth, Life. Jesus was a Person. This can be seen as Individual; but also as one in relation to others. Hegel said: 'The essence of person is to surrender oneself to the other and find fulfilment precisely in the other.'

Jesus accepts us warts and all – that is part of human relating.

Look at the incident of Sinful Woman (Lk 7:36-50) at the house of Simon the Pharisee. Jesus liberated her from her feelings of inferiority and gave her back her self-esteem.

When we look at the gospels we find qualities of friendship, affection, faithfulness and support in the relationships of Jesus. Pray about this by considering his relationship with Peter, taking a series of incidents involving his Call (Lk 5:1-11), his profession of faith (Mk 8:27-30), his denials of Jesus (Lk 22:54-62), and their reconciliation at the Lake of Tiberias (Jn 21:15-19). Through all this their friendship matured, to the point when Peter was willing to die for love of his friend.

Or consider the relationship of Jesus to his mother, Mary. She knew him as no other did. He was obedient to her and Joseph. At Cana he relied on her sense of the needs of the household. He came first to her in the Resurrection. Did he get his understanding of women because his genes were only hers? Yet their relationship was not all sweetness and light. Some expressions in the gospel seem to allow scant respect in the way Jesus treated her, appealing to another authority than hers at the age of 12 when he deliberately stayed behind in the temple though he knew she would be grieved; dealing shortly with her, telling the crowd that they were more important to him than she was.

Did Jesus have an affectionate side to his nature? The relationship with Mary Magdalene seems to be of that nature. If we are to take his humanity seriously we have to allow that his relationships were not just 'one-way'. But love has to allow freedom to change.

The relationship with Martha, Mary and Lazarus was of a particularly appealing kind. Their home was for him a kind of drop -in-when-you-can house where Jesus was always welcome and where he could put his feet up.

The relationship with John the apostle was obviously of a special kind, recognised by the other apostles.

Dwell upon these relationships of Jesus in prayer, and by doing so enrich your own relationship with him.

*Supplementary text*: 1 Sam 20: Jonathan and David.

# CHAPTER 4

# 'I to Earth'

## My relationship to the world

There is a continuity within discontinuity between the human and non-human creation. Man (Adam) is created out of the dust of the earth (Adama), of the same stuff as the rest of creation, yet with a spiritual essence shining with those clouds of glory that reflect other origins. In the interests of our domination of nature we have so long insisted on the discontinuity between the human and the rest of nature that we cannot put Humpty back together again. Or only with difficulty. Human and non-human share a common Artificer. They are the work of the same artist. The techniques and colours of one are recognisable in the other.

Darwin, so long the arch-enemy of the bible, at least had the effect of throwing man back to his organic place in nature. Whereupon the human race, ever eager to swing to extremes, having lost the body in the interests of the soul, now proceeded to overthrow the soul to advertise the body. Perfect marriage seemed to be out of the question; either the body, or the soul, but not both. Even in our spirituality of today we find the tendency to discount the body in the interests of the soul.

Rationality became the dividing sword, the cleaver, to distinguish man from the sub-human. In the process any respect for that which is non-human was lost and the relationship of our race to the earth became one of domination instead of mutual respect and wonder. The Wonders of the World became Commercial Prospects subject to Market

Forces. Some have attributed this to God's intention in the bible by giving the human being 'dominion' over the beasts and birds and things of the earth. Isn't it rather the 'dominion' of a parent over a child, involving respect, love and responsibility?

Within the physical laws everything in the universe is what it is by virtue of its relatedness to everything else. True, there is a difference between person and world and, as we have seen, attempts have been made to simplify our existence in the world by eliminating spirit or trying to promote it at the expense of our bodily well-being.

If we look back to the nature of God we should avoid these extremes. God is Three and God is One. God is both Individual Person and a Being whose meaning is in Another. God is Love and Relationship. Love and Relationship are practically synonymous. It is the relationships of God that permeate creation. We can expect then to find the tensions of relationship between different elements of creation present in our being and life. Relationship, not division, is the nature of God and therefore of creation. Everything is what it is and not another thing, but it is what it is by virtue of its relation to other things.

We are part of a network of relationships in and with the natural world around us.

To gain a right perspective on our being we have to come back again and again to the fact that we are part of creation. So much of spirituality stresses our separateness as a path to God, as though God were not present in creation. 'God is in his heaven and all is right with the world' it says. Perhaps we should be saying, 'God is in the earth and so all is right with heaven'.

At the beginning of the Spiritual Exercises St Ignatius says simply 'We are created.' He then spells out his view of what we are created for. But it must stem from that original recognition of our createdness. We are, as Rahner puts it, 'children of the earth'. So many people who come on retreat are seeking to extricate themselves from the cycle of life, from the demands of the body and the earth. Yet this is our God-given existence, this concern with birth and death, with food and home and family, this simple (did I say 'simple!'?) task of being human. The Earth is where we are made for.

How easily such a statement can be misinterpreted and condemned as materialist. We have been brought up to consider Spirit and Matter as opposed to one another. And indeed they are different. Yet the material creation is just as much of God as the spiritual.

St Thomas referred to the soul as the form of the body, rightly together as one, acting as one, in the world of material reality, giving glory to God in the splendour of earthly creation. To think of the soul as a ghost in a machine, wrongly imprisoned there and struggling to get out, is to cast a terrible slur on God's motives in making us, and a searing criticism of his capability as a creative inventor! And to think of the Christian life as a pilgrimage through hostile and tempting territory with our eyes cast down so as not to notice the beauty of the world around us lest we be seduced by it is a gross travesty of God's intention.

Those who condemn the flesh simply as a source of temptation and corruption and nothing else, should recall the old Latin tag: 'Caro cardis salutis' – the flesh is the hinge of salvation. It is through the flesh that our salvation was wrought, not despite it. And it is in and through creation that God makes himself known to us.

I say this because I fear that 'Dualism' has bedevilled our thinking and spirit for centuries and still does. It is rightly condemned as heresy because it divides God from what he has made and turns his loving creativity against himself. It is pernicious in that it is so difficult to shake off. Is there not a suspicion of it in the writings of the great Augustine himself perhaps a relic of his days as a Manichee?

In this ancient way of thinking there are two Creators, not one, a good and bad, the former creating Spirit which is good, the latter responsible for Matter which is bad. The body, of course, is in the second category and is evil. If we are to attain union with God we need to shake loose of the body and the world, and cleave only to the things of the Spirit. The Devil, the World and the Flesh were lumped together in the old catechism as sources of evil and temptation, and of the three the Flesh was probably regarded as the most dangerous! Poor old flesh! I'm sure God thought he had made a good thing when he invented flesh, and we spend so much time denigrating it.

The bible account of Genesis totally contradicts dualism. As God created the (material!) world he looked at it and saw that it was good, not bad. Not part of the devil, the world and the flesh at all!

Place yourself on the roof of a building near Joppa along with Peter who was journeying to Caesarea in answer to a call from a Roman centurion named Cornelius (Acts 10:9-18). Try to think into Peter's mind as he settles down for a siesta on a corner of the roof. He is worried about going to the house of a Gentile, since he is a Jew and commerce with Gentiles is forbidden. As for admitting them into the Christian Church...

Peter has a vision. A great sheet is let down from heaven by the four corners, full of all kinds of beasts and creepy-crawlies, and the voice of God saying, 'Up and eat!' Try to imagine the revulsion inside Peter at such a suggestion. He had been brought up strictly in the rules of eating, never touching the sorts of food considered to be 'unclean'. Now here was God apparently asking him to eat against the rules! 'No way!' says Peter in disgust, 'I never ate anything unclean!' God does not answer, 'Ah, good man, I was only testing you!' No, he takes him up on it and replies, 'Don't you call unclean what I have made and cleansed.'

Then the messengers came from Cornelius to ask him

to come quickly. As you pray this try to see in the sheet whatever it is that you feel is 'not of God' in creation.

Creation is the stepping stone to God. We live and act in and through creation, we are fulfilled in it and find God in it. In and through creation we experience the love of the creator. All down the ages people have experienced God in the things of nature. We have become used to a scientific and non-religious outlook on the universe. This has had great benefits in producing a surge in scientific invention and discovery. But at a great price, because God has been dismissed from his own land. Yet he cannot be so dismissed and is there to be seen by those with faith. As Eliade showed, the same earth is seen by faith and non-faith in totally different ways, sacred and profane.

In the eyes of faith this world, a product of God's creative love, is seat and centre of God's loving action. The very being of the universe is an epiphany, a showing forth and making known of God's presence and goodness. Ancient tribes derived strength and power fror sacred objects and places and we too attach special signifi ance to certain places such as churches and shrines. They seem to act as lightning conductors for the power from above. But for Post-Resurrection Man the whole world is redolent of God's presence and action.

Which is more 'real'? A sacred world, from which we derive being and power, or a profane one which is just what it is?

Sacred and profane are two modes of living in the world. For a person of no faith ordinary actions such as reading, sleeping, excreting, washing and so on, are simply functions of the body and no more. For a person of faith such acts, performed within a God-created cosmos, can never be simply physiological, but have a sacramental character, they convey the life and goodness of God.

To speak of a sacramental attitude to the earth gives a tremendous breadth to our ability to find God in all things.

It allows God into the very crevices of our being. Sacraments are traditionally material things, words, oils, bread, wine, water and so on, which convey the sacred to us. God comes to us in and through that which is material. Because of his commitment to creation that is his chosen path, chosen from the beginning of creation and continuing to this day. This sacredness is in the very structure of the world as transmitted to us by God.

Spiritual reality is revealed and yet concealed by the physical substance of the world. For a person of faith, material reality is not opaque, but allows the spiritual to be present. If we enter into communion with creation, if we are attentive we can discover our graced moments. Watching the water of the sea reaching out to the horizon we become aware of something unending and eternal. Gazing at a dead plant we know vulnerability and transcendence. One day in our grounds I stood beneath the aged boughs of a massive chestnut tree. It was gnarled and scarred, with broken and healed stumps and lumps. As I stood there looking up into its branches I had a strong sense of being in the arms of a mother or nurse. 'It is old earth's groping towards the steep heaven whom she childs us by' as Hopkins put it. We see the infinite in our wonder at what is finite. We never see only what we see but pass beyond it.

St Ignatius had a wonderful vision at the river Cardoner in northern Spain, a vision that integrated and made clear the whole of reality for him. When statements appeared in the rules he was writing for his new order his companions often said to him, 'Where did that come from?' and he would reply, 'The Cardoner'. Yet what was this vision? It seems to have been simply the light of the sun on the surface of the river, nothing more than that.

Nature then seems to have this wonderful ability to point beyond itself, to carry the divine.

Near our retreat house there is a roundabout, one of those massive race-tracks into which feed both directions of a motorway, two trunk roads and a new dual-carriage-way link road. They are in process of building another dual-carriageway link road. We are surrounded by strips of tarmac which are getting wider and wider. It would almost be quicker to cover the whole area with the stuff. The result is a gradual loss of contact with mother earth. In this way an essential part of that connectedness which represents our sharing in the divine life is being eroded. When the poet Hopkins exclaims in wonder: 'The world is charged with the grandeur of God' he then asks, 'Why do men now not reck his rod?' and goes on to explain, 'The soil is bare now, nor can foot feel, being shod.'

'Being shod' our contact with the earth is at one re-move. Somehow we do not live fully in the world but fleetingly, disjointedly, and cut off from a life source. Naturally it is a life-source since it mediates the life of God to us. For the same reason it is also a Nurse and a Healer. For the care-torn person there is nothing more healing than contact with the earth.

The earth has its own pace. To enter into its peace we have to adopt its pace. If you go to stay on a Hebridean island you find that you are automatically 'slowed down'. There is no need to seek special effects to cure you of the insane rush of the city it happens just by being on the island. A person is drawn without effort into stillness and contem-plation, a sense of mystery and the power of healing.

Disconnection with the earth is a form of our sinfulness. It is a function, very often, of human rapacity and greed. It stems, initially, from that lack of respect for what God has created which is at the root of all loss of true relationship. When we think of the earth as simply an object put there for our use and nothing else we use it as a mine for our plundering. It no longer has value in itself, a creature put there to give glory to God.

As we saw before, where creation is an establishing of ties, sin is the breaking of them, in a real sense, decreation.

57

The relationships of God, established in creation, binding it into unity and order, are ruptured by sin, causing the chaos in human society and in the whole of creation. To be human means to be properly bonded to God, creation and others. Sin therefore is a de-humanising process. We can be properly human only when we are in right relationship. This includes our relationship to the earth and hence, we rightly say, we can sin against the earth, or rather in the way we treat creation. We cannot either put all our eggs in the material basket, nor can we pretend it is not there. If we ignore the earth, or make it an idol, we are refusing our position as created beings.

To a person of faith, however, the earth has meaning and life since it is part of God's action. God is where he acts. The world speaks of his action. The world speaks. It is meaningful. It is part of the reality which is God.

Creation is God's gift which must be returned. We are co-creators with God, working with God, with Xt, to create the world. God is working now, creating now.

I have often heard a fragment of the long forgotten
    song
and for a moment felt the Presence that will lead us on.
I've known the heavy fall of silence
    and moments of the clearest sight,
I've known you in your darkness
    and I've known you in your light.
And I know the gift is freely given, hard to understand,
And I know the gift can only be returned.
          (Tom McGuinness SJ)

The famous letter of Chief Seattle to the President, apocryphal though it may be, is yet a beautiful statement of the respect for the earth which the Indians of North America had cherished for generations but which was sadly lacking in the attitude of the 'white man', representing as he did western 'civilization' which regarded the earth as a source to be exploited until the resources failed. We have become alarmed by the obvious detrimental effects of our rape of the earth, an alarm sounded by the sudden realization that if we continue in the present mode the earth will become a desert. The word 'rape' does not seem too strong. Chief Seattle speaks of the white man as a 'stranger who comes in the night and takes from the land whatever he needs.' For the Indian the earth is mother, and the sky is brother, relationship words.

Yet we cannot help the feeling that the voices raised against the exploitation are puny compared to the force driving it on, the force of wealth.

The evil at work is consumerism, which creates an ever-increasing need, an ever-wider opening of the mouth to swallow. There follows an ever-deepening plunder of the resources of earth. It does not take a university degree to realise that this cannot go on indefinitely. Yet to stop it will require such a change of attitude by our world as has not happened before, since it needs to be global.

So global, in fact, that we feel totally helpless. I may refuse to buy Nescafe or other goods that are tainted by malpractice, but what difference will that make to the changing of the world?

I can only say that we have to start somewhere. One thing I can do is to become aware, heighten my own realization of the way things are. It is surprising how opinion can be changed, gradually, by such awareness. It has changed with regard to smoking, despite the efforts of the tobacco companies to undermine the criticism. And in other spheres too.

And prayer? Is there not a lever here too, one that can lift God out of his seat to action? More things are accomplished by prayer than we are aware of. Prayer is a main force which enables me to take up a 'stance' in the matter of global awareness of environmental issues.

God's creating eye,
Rolling over this landscape
Is entranced. 'Good! Good!'
The hills, heaving to the horizon
Mass behind mass,
Hoist heather and stones into the sky.

Sweep the eye
Across these everlasting distances
And tell me who is monarch of these ranges?
Can you not feel the Spirit's moistening breath
Lingering in the glens?
This is God's home country.

God speaks landscape
In long flowing syllables,
Sentences of valleys and mountain ranges,
Whole paragraphs of trees,
Endless pages of sky.

God was talking
Landscape language aeons and aeons ago.
Before even dinosaurs roared
Or bibles were written
God was speaking creation.
It's his way of talking.
It's brilliant.

Devils set up idols
Of branches and cut stone,
Strange gods on high places
To make us fear our heritage,
The touch of sinew and bone.

We are in danger
Of losing root-room in the land,
Orphaned children of the earth,
Afraid of our own feet
And their connection with the soil.

Listen, then,
For magic God-whispers in glens,
For fertile growing worms under roots
And the snap of a crunched twig.
It's his voice.

Can you hear
The rumbling stomach of the hungry earth?
Listen! Your
Ears, your eyes, your nose, are tuned
To concert pitch, they are made
For earth's music.

God sings
On the keys of turning leaves,
On the chords of shafted air.
The hard, dry crackling of the stones
Is only his amused laughter.

God scans
Cloudscapes with my eyes,
His breath is the mistral;
He feels roughness with my hands
And makes valleys roll with his voice,
Water-streams are the gurgle in his throat.

God's blood
Is the circulatory system of the universe.
Our heart-strings move to his fingers.

Fingers of ice
Claw at the strings of the heart:
Blood solidifies and clots.
Heart stops, connections freeze solid.

Sin is disconnection.
Frozen roots die in their sap.
Nothing circulates
Except the icy veil of water
Obliterating vision.

God gasps
In horror at the raping of the earth!
Trees and children starve,
Skies are dyed black,
The forests are crying.
Disease riddles the soil
For our mother, the earth,
Is dying.

What can we do?
An impossible amalgam of earth and heaven,
Of spirit and muscle,
We try to keep the order of the stars.
Juggling between rule and freedom,
Passion and control,
Now breathing the fragrance of the bud,
Now the smoke of its burning.

We try to hold
The balance that will lead us to the core
Of our nature in God.
But greed, safety and refusal to adore
Destroy the balance.
It is the death of God.

Come and drink
If you are thirsty, without price.
The world is yours, your mother.
Love her then, listen to her music.
Let her wisdom lead you more deeply
Into the heart of God,
The heart of the universe.

*Texts that may help*:

Genesis 1: God saw it was good
Genesis 28:17: Truly Yahweh is here
Psalm 104: May God find joy in what he creates
Genesis 27:28: The blessing of earth's richness
Psalm 16 (JB version): After these they run...

# CHAPTER 5

# Sin:
# 'Disruption of Relationship'

*Love bade me welcome; yet my would drew back,*
*Guilty of dust and sin.*

How, in a good creation, did evil find entrance? It is a question we can never answer. We know only that it is there, causing disorder where creation had put order, causing disruption of that which God had seen to be good. Ignatius refers to sin as 'disordering'. God weaves the tapestry of creation, working now, as once he did, to produce and maintain the strands that weave the whole. It is his work of art and he is passionately interested in its wellbeing. When disruption enters in, he is distraught and works towards renewal; or rather, creative artist that he is, he works the mistake until it produces something new.

The creation bears the marks of its making. To be created is to have an inborn dynamic, a movement towards, which derives from the createdness of all things by the triune God. That direction can be diverted, towards dissolution. This does not deprive it of its being (only the Creator can do that) but causes loss of integrity.

The creature is ordered to the completion of its particular end in space and time; but this can be subverted. Redemption then becomes necessary as a re-creation.

We sin by failing to live according to our nature and being. When Jesus in the gospel imposed on humankind the apparently impossible command, 'Be perfect as your heavenly Father is perfect' (how can the finite, created being hope to become as perfect as the Creator?) it was the fulfilment of our human destiny that he was looking for, not an abstract 'perfection'. When the words are seen in their original form it is obvious that perfection implies fulfilling the end for which one is made. In being fully human we fulfil the end for which we were made. This can happen in four main areas corresponding to the four areas of our relationships:

(a) relation to God
(b) relation to others
(c) relationship within my own self
(d) relationship with the earth and the rest of creation.

The story of Adam and Eve is a demonstration of the sundering of all four sets of relationships. Their desire to be as Gods resulted in a denial of God's dominion over them, and so they disobeyed him. The result was a fear and confusion within themselves (they hid from God, feeling they were naked); they were now at odds within their own relationship resulting apparently in male domination; they were at odds with the earth itself having now to work at the earth for sustenance. And of course the relationship to God was sundered and had to be redeemed.

The breaking of the fundamental bonds of relationship is of massive consequence to the cosmos. It is not a superficial or accidental matter but causes a disruption at the heart of creation. It undoes the very work of God, is, in the deepest sense, contrary to his work and being. When we dismantle relationship we are dismantling our very essence, which stems from God and his being. His being is Love which is expressed in and through another in love. That being is transmitted into ours at creation.

Let us look at the areas of disconnection caused by sin.

We shall come back to them more fully later but now let us look broadly at the whole area.

First of all, disconnection with God. Sin, we were told, kills the soul. That is, it destroys the life of the soul. Since God is the source of that life it is not surprising that a severing of the relationship severs also the source of the life. The branch cut off from the stem withers because the sap no longer flows through it.

This happens fairly obviously when we directly defy or disobey God. That is familiar to us and scarcely needs emphasis. But failure in relationship may be more a matter of non-use than abuse. We can refuse to enter into relationship, denying the creativity of God and possibility of our own. Or we can distort it.

Is there not a failure in a refusal to acknowledge God? This is a failure in due reverence and love. A parent whose child does not acknowledge him or her is grieved because the output of their love is not responded to fully. Acknowledgement of course can be more or less explicit. There are millions of people in the world who do not acknowledge God explicitly, yet by their deeply humane responses to conditions in their world they exhibit a sense of God's presence and goodness, often more fully than many who profess a faith. Such people are acknowledging God without explicit credos. Can their lack of explicit acknowledgement of him constitute sin?

Yet it is surely a sinful failure if God is not acknowledged and given the place in our universe that is rightly his. Thereby results distortion. When God is displaced idolatry takes his place. Nowadays it is hardly the making of images of gods but the setting up of material things to worship and make the centre.

We seem to need something at centre to worship, whether it be our work or shop or fast car or house. Power has always been worshipped and wealth likewise, and, dare I say it, religion.

We read a great deal these days about False Images of God. Such false images can be a form of disconnection from God himself. If your image of your husband or wife is wrong, and you live out of that way of seeing him or her, then your relationship will be false. That will be true even if you have an artificially enhanced view of the other which does not correspond to reality. It will lead to falsehood and ultimately to disenchantment.

With images of God the same must be true, though in his case what is a right or wrong image is much more debatable, since there seems to be evidence to support all the wrong images that we want to condemn! There are plenty of passages in the Old Testament to furnish us with a God who is Policeman and Authoritarian and Revengeful as well as a God who is Loving and Parent and Mother. There is no doubt that different individuals adopt different ways of seeing God and that the way they image him will make a great difference to their outlook on life. The man whose God is always seeking for sacrifice and blood will be unlikely to invite that God into the parties and bright spots of his life.

R.S. Thomas's poem, *Ivan Karamazov*, describes God as an 'impossible robot', responding automatically – and negatively – to all our requests and prayers.

Ruth Burrows describes an incident in her autobiography in which her beautiful young sister Helen died, and for many years after she saw God as the one who removed whatever you love in your life!

Such images are taken in with our mother's milk, and are imbibed at school or home, wittingly or unwittingly. Being early learned they are hard to remove.

Here again it will come down to a stance, a discernment of where life is to be found for me. 'I have set before you life or death, blessing or curse; choose life, then, that you and your descendants may be full of life.' So God tells us in the Book of Deuteronomy (30:19). Choose life. It is a matter of discernment and choice. And what criteria can I use for such a choice? What do I use? As we said, there is evidence in Scripture for all sorts of Gods. The clue again can be found in that same chapter of Deuteronomy. 'What I ask of you this day is not something difficult or esoteric or beyond you. It is not a matter of revelation that needs a guru to bring to you from heaven, nor is it a mystery from the east that needs a wise man to tell you so that you can act on it. No. This word is so near to you that it is in your own mind and heart and mouth for you to keep.'

As in all discernment it is necessary for us to observe the effects on us of our perceptions and actions. If a particular image of God stunts my growth into full humanity then it is not good for me. When I see that thinking of God in this or that way causes desolation then I know it is the work of the bad spirit and has to be rejected. When, however, the image of God I am living allows me freedom and growth and love, then I know it to be a bringer of consolation. This is not, however, a matter of simply 'feeling good' but rather of rightness.

I realise there are presumptions at work here. I am opting for Christ's image of God rather than that of the Old Testament when the two do not seem to coincide. For Jesus, God is father, Abba. I assume that God is love and desires our growth in relationship and integrity. A 'good' image of God is one that enables that to happen; and a 'bad' image is one that thwarts such growth.

Sin causes disconnection within my own self. Read the classic text of Romans 7:14: 'I do not understand my own behaviour. The evil that I would not is what I do, the good that I see to be done I do not do.' It is a description of disruption within the self, a division pulling the self apart. Original sin is here described, not just as a past disorientation, but a present reality. The strange thing is that I seem to 'find' the tendencies within me. I do not sow them there deliberately, I find them. They are there already. I seem to have inherited them! I do not CAUSE them as far as I can see. Sin is waiting at the door for me.

When such feelings are strong it is easy to succumb to a sense of being no good. This is easily mistaken for feelings of guilt. There is a right and a wrong guilt. What I call 'wrong' guilt is a generalised feeling of 'I'm no good', not attached to any particular action. This is a psychological state of mind rather than anything to do with guilt. No matter what I do, it seems to tell me, God will not accept me. Feelings of guilt of this sort are always wrong.

True guilt is the acknowledgement that I have done wrong. It is the result of a definite action or attitude. The resulting feeling attached to it is sorrow, not guilt feelings. We may assume that when we shed tears they are necessarily a sign of sorrow. But they can be good or bad. Good tears are from genuine sorrow for wrong done, for having hurt somebody; but bad ones stem from a sense of being a rotter, and 'surely I couldn't be as bad as that!'

Mark 2:1-12: The Paralytic is a symbol of sin. In the first week of the Spiritual Exercises there is a 'composition of place': 'See in imagination my soul as a prisoner in this corruptible body and consider my whole being as an exile here on earth, cast out to live among brute beasts.' The paralysis of sin prevents normal functioning of relationships.

Jesus was concerned about sin. So much is obvious. He was concerned at the distortion caused by sin, and the rupturing of the relationship with God caused by it. But he saw that rupturing of human bonds as mediating the break with God. The Pharisees reckoned the bonds with God to be tied by means of the law, directly. Everything had to be subordinated to that. Breaking the law, in any minute detail, meant severing the tie with God. For them, the tie with neighbour was of less account. For Jesus, the person came first, and the relationship with neighbour was paramount. If you went to offer sacrifice in conformity to the law, and

70

remembered that you had a grievance with your brother or sister, then you had to go and see to that first. Because, for Jesus, in that very bond between you and your brother or sister was the love of God. That bond is the relationship of God in the Trinity, expressed into creation.

There is a striking paradox in the gospels where sin is concerned. We are told to 'sin no more', yet it is obvious from several incidents in the gospel that it is the person who has sinned, and not in lightweight fashion either, who gains a greater depth of insight into the forgiveness and love of God. The Prodigal Son, who has gone away, spent his money on debauchery ('he and his women!') and then returned because he needed food is nevertheless feted and given the ring and the robe and the sandals, all symbols of favour and authority. The elder brother, meanwhile, who has not sinned but kept the rules, turns out grumpy and resentful. It appears that the person who has had some experience of the vagaries of life stands a much better chance of knowing his need of forgiveness than the one who has stood on the touchline of life for fear of getting injured on the pitch! Again, in the encounter between the sinful woman in Luke 7, Jesus recounts a parable to Simon the host who was muttering in the background that if Jesus knew 'who this woman was' he wouldn't let her touch him. It was so simple as to be naive: two debtors, one owing a vast amount to the creditor, the other owing a small sum. The creditor lets them both off. Which debtor is going to love him more? Obviously the one who owed most. So the person who sins most is the one who loves God most who forgives him. Moral: go out and sin a lot and build up a good debt so that you will love God more! Not exactly the sort of thing one can preach from the pulpit, and we know it doesn't quite work as simply as that. A little matter of repentance gets in the way. But there does seem to be something in the parental attitude which turns a mild eye when the teenage son goes out to 'sow his wild oats'.

Thornton Wilder (in *Ides of March*) seems to capture a truth when he says: 'Wickedness may be the exploration of one's liberty. It can be a search for a limit that one can respect. A great deal of what we call "wickedness" may be the very principle of virtue exploring the laws of its own nature.'

Again, when you examine the gospel you find something of an anomaly in Jesus' attitude to the sinner. He did not seem to rate them equally. He hated all sin as evil and destructive of the work of his Father. But confronted with a person whose sin was one of weakness he was compassionate and lenient. This was particularly so where the sin was a wrong relationship. Perhaps where he saw that a person was seeking love in a distorted way the love covered a multitude of sin. He hated addiction simply because it bound a man or woman and left them unfree. It left them less than human; and the enhancement of all that is truly human was the preoccupation of Jesus.

The contrast is seen in his treatment of the Pharisees. Here was a particular kind of sinfulness that he would not tolerate. They used religion, which should have been the best expression of God's love, to tie burdens, and place people into a totally wrong relationship with God and one another. The Sabbath observance was a case in point. The Pharisees and Scribes made it a time of law-keeping. For Jesus it should have been a time when we are free to do good to each other, and be more fully human. Only those who come to the law through love can fully understand it and use it properly.

The aspect of pharisaicism that even Jesus could not touch was their attitude to God and others. They were impregnable, simply because they did not recognise that they were sinners. The law protected them from God, since keeping the law rendered them sinless (according to them). Hence they had no need of forgiveness, and so, it seemed, they had no real need of God. It was this attitude which

Jesus saw as the worst kind of sin since it was so untouchable, unforgivable. Only sin which is acknowledged can be forgiven; or rather, only when the forgiveness is acknowledged is it effective.

Imagine yourself as the Pharisee (Luke 18:9-14) going into the temple (or your local church) to pray, and you stand or kneel at the back and thank God for all the good things you have got. Then you notice, at the front, a well-known alcoholic standing in the aisle, leaning against one of the benches, dishevelled and dirty. What thoughts go through your mind?

To love God is to do his will, to obey him, to observe the commandments. 'If you love me you will keep my commandments.' And when we look at what God demands of us it is in the realms of creating the earth and human society in his image. What God seems to point to as sin on earth is the failure to love our brothers and sisters in the deepest sense of that word love.

You cannot love the God you cannot see if you do not love the person you can see. So love of God and of neighbour are inextricably bound up together. As we saw, the Judge in Matthew 25 separated the goats and sheep by the simple criterion of how each had treated neighbour.

Why do we so often fail the test, fail to show love to the other person in need? Ill-will often enough, but also sheer lack of observation.

Consider the story of Dives and Lazarus. There is no evidence there of Dives dealing drastically with Lazarus, kicking him or calling the police to take him away, or having him knifed by thugs. He simply did not notice him. Occupied with his own table, and his house and affairs, he scarcely saw the beggar on his own doorstep. In the eyes of the gospel such lack of sight is sinful and, literally, damnable. It is a complete failure in respect for the other, in recognising him as a human being with dignity and need.

'As often as you do this to the least of these you do it to me', said Jesus.

The sin of severing of relationship occurs so often in our society that it forms the bread and butter of tabloid newspapers. We read of it in the break up of marriages, in family squabbles, in communities with petty rivalries, jealousy, manipulation, judging others, failing to support others on the principle of pushing them down so you go up; failure to support or praise or affirm.

Traditionally we have viewed sin as a personal thing, a wrongdoing in the individual breast. Nowadays we are realising more and more the corporate nature of sinfulness. The disruption of relationship is seen on a large scale when nation goes to war with another nation and hatred replaces love. Or within a nation where sectarianism gives rise to racial strife. What caused Jesus most anger and even violence was injustice of any sort. Injustice is a form of wrong relationship of power. The voice of God raised against any unjust dealings was familiar enough to the Jews, for they had listened to it time and time again in the Prophetical writings. They had heard it when John the Baptist called some of his listeners a 'brood of vipers'. Jesus himself attacked the Scribes and Pharisees because they laid unjust burdens on people in the name of religion. He drove the buyers and sellers from the temple precincts because they too were using the name of God his Father to make extortionate profits.

The commandments demand respect for my neighbour. Any attitude which lowers my neighbour to a position in which I look down on him or her, is a sin against respect and right love. And when a relationship of love has been snapped, the work of putting that relationship right is a Christ-like act. That is why the gospel stresses the need for forgiveness since it is an essential part of the re-establishing of relationship and therefore of God's work of redemptive love.

Jesus came with healing in his hands. He healed the physical dislocations within people, their paralysis, bentness, sickness; he healed their moral disintegration, their inner dividedness; and he healed their divisions from one another by asking them to forgive. Above all he was healing the division they felt between themselves and God in heaven, by forgiving their sins. He came to remake connectedness.

All injustice is wrong relationship. It is a denial of the dignity of the other as a child of God, as bearing the God-image as fully as we do ourselves, but seeing him or her as of a lower grade than ourselves, with no rights.

When a landowner suppresses the rights of tenants or others he is adopting a sinful attitude because of a failure in recognising the need for true relationship. He has substituted a relationship of dominion and lording over for the true one of equality under God. Even before actual acts of injustice are perpetrated he is in a sinful situation. Threads of the weaver's picture have been torn out and broken.

The fourth relationship that is broken by sin is that between ourselves and the earth. God created the whole universe, not just human beings, and he looked on it with pleasure. The connectedness that is God was put into creation. Part of our essence is our connectedness with the earth from which we came. 'God took the dust of the earth and fashioned man...' is an expression of our rootedness in the world. Rootedness in the earth is not just something to make us feel good, it is part of our essence. All creation is enveloped in relationships.

The bible seems to place man in a position of exploitation with regard to the earth, in the command to subdue the earth. If this is taken literally it ignores our own createdness and dependence on the earth for part of our being. Domination represents a false relationship with the earth.

Failure in responsibility to creation is wider than simply polluting the earth. It results no doubt from a lack of wonder and understanding of the true nature of this earth as derived from God's creative love. Where there is no reflection and prayer there may well be a failure to notice God's presence in what he has created. True worship is then replaced by placing false gods at the centre of our lives, gods of materialism which are so prevalent today in our commercialised society.

Failure in a right attitude to creation can also stem from wrong images of God being allowed to lodge in our hearts and minds. When God is seen as opposed to his own creation, when he is reckoned to rule by fear rather than love, and when his influence stultifies growth rather than promoting it, then we can be sure we are dealing with an anti-god.

The most obvious crime against creation on our part is the waste and destruction of the gift of creation – a global responsibility which we are becoming aware of increasingly today. The Welsh poet, R.S. Thomas, talks of 'poisoning with fertilisers the place where the child lay'.

In his book, *The Cosmic Covenant*, Robert Murray SJ shows that buried in the bible are references to a covenant between God and Creation, right from the start. It emphasises the deep connection between ourselves and the earth and warns of the consequences of violation of that covenant. Isaiah 24 provides a typical example:

> See how Yahweh lays the earth waste,
> makes it a desert, buckles its surface,
> scatters its inhabitants,
> priests and people alike, master and slave.
> Ravaged, ravaged the earth,
> despoiled, despoiled.
> The earth is mourning, withering,
> the world is pining, withering,
> the heavens are pining away with the earth.
> The earth is defiled under its inhabitants' feet,

for they have transgressed the law, violated the
   precept,
broken the everlasting covenant.
So a curse consumes the earth
and its inhabitants are burnt up
and few are left.

Disconnection with the earth is at once a neglect of our
connectedness and a deliberate violation or rather exploitation of the resources of the earth. Thus it takes on the aspect
of rape. Yet we can be blissfully unaware of it! In order to
heighten awareness of our own part in the pollution that is
gradually choking us try an imaginative exercise. See a
little stream running along behind a factory, and into the
stream the factory is pouring chemicals resulting from its
manufacturing processes. See the stream flowing to join a
bigger one which has also been polluted from other sources.
This larger stream is joined by another and another and
then flows into a large river which receives not only chemi-
cal waste but sewage. This flows into the sea. The whole
area of the sea at that point is polluted. In this way you
build up a sense of how, from small beginnings something
gross can result.

*Other texts that may help*:

   Genesis 3: The Fall
   Genesis 4: Cain and Abel
   Genesis 6:5-8: God grieved
   Psalm 16: (JB version) 'My Princes!'
   Isaiah 44:9-20: A satire on idolatry
   Romans 7:14-25: The evil that I would not, I do.

# CHAPTER 6

# Who is this...?

## *The One I follow*

Christ came to claim his own, to be with his family.

But at his coming he found his mission was to save, to reassert the rule of God in our hearts and form again the bonds that God had once established. He came to repaint God's lovescape.

St Ignatius puts before us the ideal of the King, attractive and compelling, as a figure of Christ. Alas, kings are sapped of meaning, if not positively discredited from their long history of power-seeking and corruption. Let us simply stand before Jesus himself.

Walk, then, alongside Jesus as he journeys towards the ancient seat of pagan and Roman religion at Caesarea Philippi. Here was an apt place to discuss the significance of the Christ. Sit with the resting group by some stream or outcrop of rocks and hear Jesus say: 'What's the general opinion? What are people saying about me?' Hear them tell him the various tales whispered on the wind, that he is John the Baptist returned, a prophet come with power to judge, and so on. Then he catches your eye with the challenge: 'And YOU Jim (Joan, Jack, Jane or Josh) who do YOU say I am?'

Thus, in prayer, I ask myself what I really think of Christ Jesus, who is he, what is his real significance in my life? Only the strictest honesty can reply, the answer given by the Spirit deep within me. No book knowledge will suffice nor the slick phrases of the catechism. They may have helped form my infant faith, but now I meet the source himself and must struggle to reply. Would it really make a difference if he were not there? And if he does count, truly, in my life, what is it that he means to me?

I might have to admit that the Christ I have been brought up with is a very nebulous character, or an unknowable one. I may have to admit that the person I learn about in the gospel is not so easy to believe in, or is a bit of a mixture. I am told he is both God and man, and find that I cannot easily put the two together because the man in Jesus is overshadowed by the God in Jesus to such an extent that I don't fully believe in his humanity.

It has been said that the whole meaning of Jesus' coming to our earth was simply to be human and to give the fullest and deepest expression to human existence. His need to learn as a child and boy, though a diminishment of his Godhead, was never a curb to fruitfulness.

Can I really read the gospels without being bugged by the feeling that he knew everything anyway because he was God? When things got difficult in his public life he could simply 'slip away' because 'his time' had not come. This is not the fate of a normal human being. And could he not avoid or sidestep any human circumstance that was not according to the divine 'plan'? If he had wanted to he could have come down from the cross. And so, no matter how we try, we find his humanity being sidestepped and undermined by his divinity.

The apostles encountered Jesus in just the opposite way from us. They met him first as a man, albeit a rather extraordinary and attractive one. Only gradually, through reflecting on their experience of being with him, did they come to the astonishing conclusion that he stood in a special relationship to God the Father. We, on the other hand, if we are brought up as Christians, are familiar with him as the God-Man. We see him as God somehow given a human body. The result is that we never really encounter him as a human being, and the Incarnation becomes a kind of miracle-trip organised by God to remind us that our eyes should be focused on heaven, not earth.

Such an attitude is a travesty of the Incarnation. The church struggled in the early years to avoid any suggestion that Christ's humanity was not real or full. He wasn't play-acting. And if he wasn't, then, in order to experience the full reality of being human, he must have known dependence, vulnerability, joy, surprise and other components of our living.

The difficulty is compounded, I know, by the fact that Jesus seemed to have missed out on two very usual factors of human experience. He never sinned, and he never had a sexual life. As God he could not sin. Since that is so, then he could surely not experience real temptation, because, if there is no possibility of succumbing, how real can a temptation be? Certainly he could experience difficulty and counter-attraction but never with the real possibility of sin. He never had a sexual life. Or so it would seem, from the gospels. So he missed out on a very normal component of human living. The horrified reaction to Scorsese's film (*The Last Temptation*) is evidence enough of our conviction of that and our listing sexuality among the sins!

It brings us back to our contemplation of Jesus. Who do we say that he is? How do we know him? As friend, or God, or superman? What is he all about?

In the second week of the Spiritual Exercises we spend some time contemplating the life of Christ. Although we are open to whatever occurs when we pray, nevertheless it seems that Ignatius had something in mind. We are invited to seek into the deep mystery of the emptying of God, the so-called 'kenosis' of Phil 2:6-11.

Though he was of divine form, he didn't try to cling on to his being of the God form but gave up all that and became a slave, became as we are, human.

That is our challenge too, to strip off the trappings of divinity in our assumptions about Jesus, in order to experience with him, in contemplation, what it was to become human and be with us, not in pretence, but in reality. We can only do this by staying with the gospels and allowing them to speak to us.

The Nativity, for instance, at the beginning of the second week of the Spiritual Exercises, is not there to enhance the jingle-bells and robins and the carols. Rather is it a contemplation of the stark reality, outlined in Phil 2, of what it meant for God to become human.

We are invited to enter the cave or stable, be present totally, using our senses in imagination. We see who is there and what is done, we hear what is said, and even what we ourselves are saying, we smell the hay or dung, we touch the cold side of the cave. We contemplate the mystery of this baby. Every baby is a mystery, but this one encapsulates the profound fact of spirit in matter, God enfleshed. The mystery is all the more extraordinary for being so ordinary. Only the simple eyes of shepherds, close to the earth, could see the wonder in the flesh. Of all the young of the animal kingdom the human baby is perhaps the most helpless for longest.

So the first lesson in being human seemed to be total dependence. God became dependent on the care and goodwill of his own creation, a contrast to King David's choice when he attempted to hold a census of his people. God took exception to this and offered David a choice of penance. 'Which do you want: three years of famine, three months of being ravaged by your enemies, or three days of pestilence from God over the whole land?' David found it a hard choice but decided on the pestilence from God's hand, because, as he said, 'I'd prefer to fall into God's hands for he is merciful, and not into the hands of men!' – for they are not!

Yet here, when God himself is deciding how to deal

with us he seems to decide the other way – to place himself totally into the hands of us people, and our world and circumstances. If he does that he is no longer in control of those circumstances. The very essence of his choice is precisely in being vulnerable to the pressures of being human. To be human is to be unable to control circumstances, or only to a limited degree. For God to place himself into the 'hands of men' was to take a great risk.

What if the human race did not accept him? 'He came to his own and his own received him not.' I believe that this vulnerability, this helplessness went even further. Christ was at the mercy of human circumstances and not just human beings. It was a Roman census, held no doubt for political or economic reasons, that caused Joseph to travel to Bethlehem. The birth was subject to the normal risk of such things. There were no maternity hospitals and infant mortality was great. What if he had died at birth? What if he had caught a chill or caught pneumonia (as a sister of mine did in her babyhood and died)? What, indeed, if Herod's soldiery had caught up with the couple and the baby had joined the massacre? What if!? Is it useless to speculate in this way? We know what did in fact happen. There are no 'might-have-beens' with God, as one of my fellow Jesuits says. I ask the 'what ifs' simply to bring home the stark reality of what it meant for God to be human.

So as you gaze on the baby in the manger allow yourself to wonder at this mystery of how God could empty himself of power and godhead and place himself in the womb of, and then into the care of a young girl. What a responsibility to give to a simple human being! It shows what an astonishing trust God is willing to put into creation.

Was this a way of re-establishing relationship? God placed himself into a relationship of child to mother, of helpless baby to providing parent. It is a reversal of roles, the human caring for the God. Christ was later to point, more than once, to the child as a model. Was it just to emphasise that if we are to be in relationship we must be dependent, vulnerable and trusting?

Maybe we have searched too hard to find, and separate out, the divine strain in Christ's being because we have demeaned the value of human life. In accepting the human condition God was surely pointing out to us that human life is coded with the divine imprint. Jesus came to be human. Thirty years of his thirty three were spent in doing nothing other than growing and living as a human being. Wandering round an exhibition of the industrial landscapes of L.S. Lowry I wondered whether Christ would have fitted in there.

Christ looked and saw that it was Good.
He walked the streets and shouted over shuttles,
drank beer in pubs and danced at every corner.
He roared with life, paraded with a banner
and lived full-bloodedly among his neighbours,
chanting the lays and folk-songs of his people,
mourning the deaths of mill-slaves killed in harness,
slept in a bed of bone-invading dampness,
sheltered from corroding rain and weather,
elbowed his way through jostling crowds at market.
He shared the evolution of our species
and stepped up to his neck into the River
and never doubted this was what he came for.
He saw that it was Good.
Christ was engaged, was risen in those people.

Not, perhaps our traditional picture of Christ until we remember that he was accused of being a drunkard and lay-about. His gospel message shows us a God who is passionately interested in human life and in the right relationships of respect that he originally sowed there. The reason the evangelists inveighed against riches was not that they are

84

evil in themselves but that they are used as a means of domination of those who have none. That is a distortion of the right relationships that God placed into his creation and that is why Jesus preached against it and all the evil that comes in its train.

The preaching and actions of Jesus in his public ministry bear even fuller testimony to his mission to give value to that which is human.

Imagine yourself on a hillside with a crowd of other people, listening to Jesus. You notices the intensity of the man, his incisive gestures and the burning determination in his eyes. For the things he is saying, which time would pacify and polish, are dynamite to the hearers.

The theme he is enunciating is not incidental to him, but a subject of passionate interest.

Blessed are you who are poor; yours is the kingdom.
Blessed are you hungry; you will be filled.
Blessed are you who weep; you shall laugh.
Blessed are you who are oppressed and marginalized
    because you believe in me; be glad, be joyful, the
    good times are coming.

What are your thoughts and feelings when you hear this? Are you glad, are you joyful, are you uplifted? Or are you thinking, I don't want to be poor, I don't want to be hungry, I don't want to have to weep?

Well, maybe that is because you are NOT poor or hungry or oppressed. Imagine though, that you ARE abjectly poor, hungry like the African in a drought, oppressed like many a poor peasant in South America. Here is this man telling you that you are really blessed, and, wonder of wonders, the Kingdom is yours. It is not for the managers, or the vastly wealthy, or the politicians, or the Church leaders, it is YOURS.

This, of course, is why Jesus died. He was upsetting the

status quo. He was telling the crowd of ordinary people who were kept well in check, not only by the Romans, but by their own authorities using the law of God as pretext, he was telling them that God was with THEM, not with those who were using them to maintain their own positions. That was what Romero said to the people in his country, and so he too died. Indeed, that is exactly what Jesus said would happen to anyone saying things like that! In any society the wealthy and powerful minority will always feel threatened by the ones they oppress.

Why is it that God chooses to side with the poor and marginalized and make them the owners of the Kingdom? Is it not simply that God is affronted by the inequalities and divisions in his world and he comes in power to right it? Through the Old Testament the prophets were shouting out God's wrath at injustice and the enslaving of one person by another. The relationships of creation are distorted and snapped by such behaviour. To treat another person as your slave, whether in name or by political or mercenary domination, is to cease to relate to him or her as neighbour and to make him into an object. When this is done by a government or regime to a whole class of people the evil is compounded.

One of the things Jesus announced was the Lord's Year of Favour, or the Jubilee Year. It was an ideal expressed in the Book of Leviticus to enshrine the religious conviction that God is creator and owner of the land and it is entrusted to the Israelites by covenant. The people were not owners but tenants. It emphasised the correct relationships of people to God, which would, of their nature, constitute the relationships of person to person and the person to the land. In its most primitive form it may even have implied a redistribution of the land in the year of Jubilee every 50 years, a redistribution of wealth among the whole people, irrespective of merit or moral standing. The ideal was probably never realised, but it remained an ideal.

This last aspect is a direct reflection of God's own attitude. God's grace, his forgiveness, his love, is not given as the result of our merit. If it were so, how graceful or forgiven or loved would we be?

Try to pray the story of the Labourers in the Vineyard. (Mt 20:1-16). Imagine yourself as one of those labourers who was hired early in the morning, worked hard all day in the heat and the dust, watching other later arrivals right through the day, and coming finally to queue up for payment, at the end of the line. You expect the payment to be in proportion to the hours spent working. But no, you receive exactly the same wage as the one who came near the end of the day. Yet it was in accord with the agreement with the employer. 'My friend,' says the owner, 'I do you no wrong. If I chose to give the same to these others as to you, do you begrudge me my generosity?'

God's giving is not based on our merit or virtue. We tend to make these virtues, of hard work, or duty, or lawfulness, or righteousness, the touchstones of God's will and favour. As a result of them we are in God's favour, and therefore privileged and even wealthy. In this way class oppression is based on the will of God, as of divine right. The law becomes the arbitrator and so religious correctness can be an oppressor. The oppressed may themselves conform to this way of thinking, considering that they are rightly judged and suppressed! Jesus cut clean through all this, showing that his God was not going to condone any such way of thinking. The poor of the gospel were not chosen out by God as possessors of the Kingdom because of their 'merit' but solely because they were the victims of the inequality and corruption of the right relationships which He (God) had established in his creation.

Jesus came to establish, or re-establish the Lovescape of God on earth. Sin had fragmented the wholeness of creation, had divided person from person, nation from nation. Babel signified division. Domination of one nation by another, one people by another became so entrenched in the thinking and actions of society that we in our 'civilised' west have scarcely yet shaken off its dreadful cloak. Neighbour became servant as empires were built.

With the compassion of his Father Christ looked upon his people, like sheep without a shepherd and set himself to set them free.

'I have come to be with my people, struggling under the burden of oppression and ignorance, slavery and sin, ravaged by disease and poverty. I have come to my own. I will not rest until the enemies of life are conquered and the scourge of sin removed that makes of God himself an enemy!'

Redemption is to do with relocation, reconnection. Jesus, Firstborn of creation, establishes the wholeness of the earth. He is part of the earth and the landscape, at home in it. His boyhood was spent in it. He talks of the lilies of the field, he prays in the wilderness. His heart bleeds at the brokenness of human kind. Hence his work of healing and forgiving. By healing he was mending the dislocations of sickness. By forgiving he was healing broken relationships with God, with people. The power of relationship between himself and his Father is the same as that between himself and his disciples and us, and is the same as that between people.

Jesus is the great Connector. He brings in the isolated, the marginalized, the sinners, takes them out of their isolation, back into the communion of his Father and human society.

In Christ we see the God of Compassion. We experience a God who earnestly desires that his work of love, creation, should be fulfilled and not thwarted. God is ever at work in creation mending what is broken, trying to reestablish, make anew. In sin, in injustice, in suffering and evil of every kind God finds his creation threatened. He looks with particular compassion on the victims of these destructive forces, the marginalized, the poor, the outcasts, the isolated, the oppressed.

Christ is the compassionate face of God. Hence the healing, forgiving, the saving. Hence the preaching of the Good News.

That is pre-eminently his 'brief'. When he read from the scroll in the synagogue at Nazareth and cited the words of Isaiah: 'to bring sight to the blind, let prisoners go free, make the good news known; and declare the Year of Favour' he was declaring openly what he thought he was about, his manifesto. 'This', he said, 'is being fulfilled in your sight right now.'

Nor did he allow anyone in that synagogue to be neutral about him, but confronted them with his own person. In retreat I too am confronted by the truth of Jesus, I too cannot remain neutral.

If I seek the trappings of power or reputation Christ is not for me, despite what history may have done to him. Is he a king? Yes, but not of the sort our histories tell us about. His rule is the instress of his call in the heart. His power is exercised against evil, and on behalf of the poor and powerless. His leadership is one of service, not command. This, he tells us, is what God is like.

What I am confronted by is the demand of Jesus. It is a demand that I enter into the same struggle that he entered, and by the fullness of my human life to work for the kingdom of God on earth. But the word 'Kingdom' is loaded with heavy historical chains. Better to see my commitment as, first of all, a relationship to Christ in person which inevitably involves me in his quest. I can do this by contemplating the woman at the well in John chapter 4.

It tells of a woman traipsing to the well, isolated by her own past, wanting, though she did not know how, to rise out of the doldrums of her life. She carries the symbol of her life, the empty jar, a jar made to carry life-giving water, but now dry. She does not realise that she is carrying it to Christ. She thinks that what she does is a daily chore; but that is where we meet Christ. He does not demand that they talk in church or in a special place. Where she is will do.

Christ takes the initiative. That is typical of God, the source and well of life. He asks for her help. She is asked to minister to him. Relationship has begun, one of equality, not dominance. And then begins the long journey of trust, the skirmishing that leads to openness. She cannot do it on her own. The relationship of her need is established.

She listens because of the obvious interest. There is a mutual interest which establishes the relationship. Love is shown by interest in the person rather than in the situation or 'case'. The relationship made her feel 'safe'. She can be open. She trusts him. The process of change and healing can begin.

Suddenly she has a message and a mission, to tell of this person, and what he can do. She takes on his work, telling of how she has been changed, made whole, able again to lift her head. He is now the one she will follow, because what he has done for her he can do for all, and will do so through her.

She goes with enthusiasm and desire, marks of the apostle. Commitment to Christ means working with him for this kingdom with him, alongside him, accepting what he accepts. It means weeping over Jerusalem because it refused salvation. It means trying, with the power of Christ, to bring into embrace again what was separated and re-unite what was divorced. The apostle stands for reconciliation and forgiveness.

The call is personal and continuing. It is not like a treasured jar received as a wedding-present to stand ever after on the mantelpiece, dusted reverently from time to time, but otherwise unchanged. It is a living thing. Pray the Potter in Jeremiah 18 and watch the hands of the Creator at work forming the pot, which is yourself. He is doing it now, his hands ever shaping your life. Everything changes in our lives: society, world, church, order, myself. And so the call will change, like a bird following the contours of hills in flight, the follower of Christ is ever listening for his voice, watching his hand for an indication. In other words, to use the jargon term, constant discernment. I pray to discern the call for me, and to do that I reflect on what my talents are, and how the Lord may want to use them.

*Texts to help your prayer:*

Luke 2:1-20: The Nativity
Luke 4:16-22: Call of the apostles
Ephesians 1:17-19: What hope his call holds for you
Exodus 35:30-36: Endowed with skill
Matthew 25:14-30: To each he gave talents

# CHAPTER 7

# Redeemed Relationship

## The Crucifixion

I stand on Calvary, imagining myself there. The sky is hot and leaden, I hear the sounds as though from a distance. There are people there, but I am hardly aware of them. Squatting down on the rocky surface I stare at the cross. The man there has been stripped of everything, possessions (only his coat worth anything and the soldiers have already claimed that), reputation, credibility, and dignity. He faces nothing but this inhuman death. No wonder he shouts out to heaven, 'Why have you forsaken me?' It is a cry we sometimes use when things go against us.

What are my thoughts, what are my feelings, gazing at this unfortunate being? So disfigured does he look, as Isaiah says, that he doesn't seem human any more.

No doubt the question will come: What is this all about? Why this dereliction? What had he done to deserve this? It is easy enough to reply, nothing, he had done nothing, he was innocent. But in truth he had done a great deal, and, depending on your point of view, he was far from innocent.

As I look about on the hill of Calvary I am aware of the Roman soldiers, and I am aware of the triumphant religious leaders of the time. I realise that this man on the cross had violated established norms of conduct and attitude, and had upset the religious and political establishment alike. From their point of view he had to go.

We may have been brought up with certain ways of thinking about the cross which are unhelpful. It has become the central symbol of the Christian faith. So much so that it has become cuddled and cradled as the sweet instrument of our salvation. In fact it was a devilish horror, a torture that only man could have devised. The picture of the cross in Endo's book, *The Samurai* is more telling: that emaciated figure on the cross with his head hanging down...

> I become aware of the crucified
> a hacked torso hung on a beam
> fingers clawing in spasm, eyes a-stream
> with blood, as though he cried.

We are tempted to think that God sent his son to this death. Could a good God perpetrate such an evil? The Passion is not entirely free of the echoes of a domineering Father ruling his son. Yet we cannot blame this on God; it was man's doing, the hatred of humans like us. The way laid down by the Father was surely not the cross, but the proclamation of the truth which involved the cross.

Jesus did it for his Father. It was the inevitable outcome of his life and preaching. It follows directly from the preaching of kingdom that became the obsession of Jesus' life. He desperately wanted to bring a world where peace, love, openness, godliness reigned. Thy kingdom come on earth. But he could not do that without at the same time condemning roundly the sinful tendencies in human society which undermined such a kingdom.

His war of words with the Pharisees resulted from their making of religion into a law-load to weigh people down. He joined the prophets of the Old Testament who shouted angrily against all forms of hatred, division, ungodliness in the structures and measures of society.

What Jesus was standing for, and dying for, was not a political system but God. To do that he had to side with those who were oppressed by the system, and hence he wanted to change it. As a result the system denounced him, told him he was subversive, and execrated by God. Early in his public life he was cast out of the synagogue in the name of religion. He died cursed, spat upon and abandoned; yet beloved by and taken to the arms of God. In this way the Lord confounds the wisdom and justice of the world.

It becomes apparent then that the cross is not a sacred idol but a violation and rejection of the rights of God and human beings. The work of Christ strived to remove it from the face of the earth. The cross is not a positive value in itself. Hence the paradox, that those who accept the cross do so in order to wipe its evil from the earth, and establish the reign of God to the extent that the cross could not happen. The need for it, the cause of it, should be removed. But it can only be removed by taking it up, for by doing so the logic of hatred is broken. 'To accept the cross is to be greater than the cross.' Death, the instrument that hatred uses to break the power of good, is in fact defeated by itself.

The cross is an extreme act of love, trust and total self-abnegation. Jesus transfigured suffering and death into acts of liberty and love, into a new approach to those who were rejecting him. He offered pardon, and entrusted himself to God. Pardon is the truest measure of love. Pardon and confidence are the ways we avoid letting hatred and desperation have the final word. It is the supreme gesture of all that is great in human nature. Thus death is given an ultimate meaning.

It is for God that Christ died, not for any political system. Hanging there on the cross Jesus looked about him. This was his own country, these were his own countrymen and women. These were the people he had tried to help, to liberate. It was for them he had traipsed the countryside, it was these hands, now pierced, that had blessed them and their children, these feet, now lacerated, that had gathered the dust of the roads on their behalf. Yet they had crucified him, given him over to the very power they hated and despised, the Romans.

Imagine that you stand up and move slowly over to the cross and stand beneath it and look up.

'Why?' you ask, 'Why have they done this to you?'

'Why? Because I opposed their sin with God's justice, because I told them the truth of God. Know this: if you stand for justice in the world, if you witness to God's truth and to me you will walk the way of the cross along with me, and you will suffer with me.'

Those who struggle for justice are witnesses to God and to Christ. They struggle with and suffer with Jesus. What are they struggling to do? To eradicate the injustice and the structures that produce it. The injustice, frequently, is built into the very structure itself, and fighting the injustice involves dismantling the structure. That in turn means being branded a revolutionary and traitor or even communist. It may involve being branded a blasphemer since the image of God they represent will oppose that of the oppressor. The one who strives for justice is trying to restructure society with a new attitude, but the forces that stand to lose by such a change, those with power and wealth, will oppose any change, will try to perpetuate the unjust system.

Being united with Christ in his suffering means solidarity with anyone who has been dehumanised and stripped of rights. It may be an active participation or it may be a solidarity of prayer and compassion. But by going against the system as established the Christian will undoubtedly be told that he is meddling in politics and should keep clear of it. Christ's death proclaims that anyone who stands for justice is thereby rendered political. Anyone who even stands for all that is human is thereby political. God cannot be excluded from any human concern, and politics is a human concern. Christ died on the cross under the ironic title, Jesus of Nazareth, king of the Jews. He was crucified as traitor and blasphemer.

There has to be a terrible confrontation between the person who wishes to follow Christ and the ideals of many of those who rule the world. What these rulers will call right and helpful and growthful is in fact wrong and unhelpful and oppressive. In proclaiming this the Christian places himself out in a very vulnerable place, in fact on the way of the cross. He loses credibility for much of the society around him, he may well lose the security of his job, and he may even, in some circumstances, put his life on the line.

To live with the cross in this way is life-giving, life springing from love, solidarity, and courage that is willing to endure and die. Death and Resurrection are inevitably found in the same bed at the same time. We can allow our Christianity to become tainted with a death wish and the somewhat masochistic flavour of certain forms of Good Friday procession. That is not the Christianity of the gospel. Rather it is a positive struggle to ensure that the wretched cross of oppression and slavery be removed from the earth.

Only love can conquer evil, and God is love. God does not stand aside from creation, indifferent to the oppression that permeates much of society. But, pace the Old Testament, God's way of removing it cannot be by the very weapons it uses, violence, fear, and vengeance, but only by love. That involves suffering the evil and pardoning the offenders.

The cross is a reality of life. It is not something imposed by God in order to sanctify us but an evil that he too sees as an impediment to the fulfilment of his kingdom.

The cross is 'folly' as St Paul says. It gives the lie to all the props and securities in our lives which support us. Religion itself, in certain ways, may constitute security and become a human assertion against the will of God. The cross is what distinguishes Christianity from other religions. It is not, or should not be, a religion of triumph and domination in this life but of acceptance of the evil.

To emphasise this, continue to stand in your imagination on Calvary just after Christ has died, a torn body stripped of everything, reputation, success, credibility (remembering that the apostles ran away).

Suffering is part of creation. Anything you love will bring suffering. Standing up for justice and truth involves the cross.

How can a good God allow such suffering? It is a question constantly asked of hospital chaplains and priests at funerals. Since God is the author of everything, is he not the author of suffering? Can he not prevent it? Why does he let a small girl be blown up by terrorist bombs? Why does he allow gang rape in Bosnia? Can he who saved so many not save himself? Christ on the cross gives no answer. In the end he said, 'Father, forgive them, they don't know what they are doing.' The cross is Christ's only response to the foulness of sin, injustice, exploitation, rape, murder and all the other horrors we see rampant in the world.

The Passion is the ultimate expression of God's love. We find in it the attraction of the redeeming love of God. It is paradoxically in the Passion that many find the pull to serve Christ. Or rather, if we take Hopkins' words as indicative, the pull towards God ('stress' is Hopkins' term) comes from the life and death of Christ:

> Not out of his bliss
> Springs the stress felt
> Nor first from heaven (and few know this)
> Swings the stroke dealt –
> Stroke and a stress that stars and storms deliver,
> That guilt is hushed by, hearts are flushed by
>     and melt –
> But it rides time like riding a river
> (And here the faithful waver, the faithless fable
>     and miss).

It dates from day
Of his going in Galilee;
Warm-laid grave of a womb-life grey;
Manger, maiden's knee;
The dense and the driven Passion, and frightful sweat;
Thence the discharge of it, there its swelling to be...

Hence, in praying the Passion, the main stress need not
be on the physical experience of the sufferings but rather
on a deep recognition of the love involved. Too much
concentration on the physical death can cause a fear of the
Passion and hence the danger of missing the great grace of
it. The cross is God's proof that he will go to any length to
heal the shattering of relationships we have caused. He
shouldered all this when he became man, all the
woundedness, the severed trust, the greed. And he called
his burden light!

The cross is the drawing power that pulls the severed
threads back together. Jesus can heal only where there is
faith, because that is the expression of trust in the healer.
Relationship is involved in the very act of healing. Compassion is the Godquality seen in Jesus and exercised in his
interactions with people. It also is a necessary quality of
relationship. It is involved especially in the contemplation
of the Passion.

When I sin I crucify the Christ in me. I paralyse him,
render him unable to move. Look again at the curing of the
paralytic in Mark 2. What paralysis does to the body sin
does to the soul.

In a mysterious way we enter into the very fabric of
God's relationship to the world when contemplating the
Passion. Christ hangs between earth and heaven as a sym-
bol of a reconnection of the two, us and God. He IS us and
God.

We can dwell on our own individual crosses or on those
of whole peoples. Our crosses may be everyday things like

parting from those we love, or like waiting on God and on events. Parting, because any growth means leaving things behind. Consider how Jesus left home after 30 years, breaking ties that meant a great deal to him. Yet if he were to mature in the spirit, fulfil his Father's will, he had to leave his mother and home behind.

Perhaps one of the difficult aspects of salvation is the idea of Christ dying for us. Or conversely the sense that we have put Christ on the cross. How can this be true? How can I have anything to do with a situation 2000 years ago? It is the realisation that my sin contributes to the whole. We do not realise what we are doing. ('Father forgive them, they don't know'). Perhaps it is fortunate that we don't.

The sense of what we do to another is conveyed strongly in Wilfred Owen's wartime poem in which a soldier, in a reverie, sees himself meeting the enemy soldier he has killed. The words could well be those of Christ to us:

Courage was mine, and I had mystery,
Mystery was mine, and I had mastery;
Then when much blood had clogged their
    chariot-wheels
I would go up and wash them from sweet wells...
I would have poured my spirit without stint.

I am the enemy you killed, my friend.
I knew you in this dark; for so you frowned
Yesterday through me as you jabbed and killed...

Sorrow and contrition are the result of knowing what we have done to another, the injury we have caused, the wife whose life we have blighted, the child whom we have made defensive and afraid, the neighbour we have demeaned as a fool. When we hear the other speak we know that their life too was precious, and full of potential. The cross will never be absent from our lives. It is built into the fabric of living.

Bearing the weight of old age, of the diminishment brought about by the gradual weakening of our faculties, these are part of the cross, though they seem so ordinary. Crosses, after all, come in varying sizes. The losing of our sharpness of memory so that we cannot remember the name of someone we know quite well may seem to be a relatively small thing, but when eventually it results in not knowing one's own kith and kin it causes dismay.

Contemplate Mary in the passion and try to be aware of the feelings of a mother who watches her child, her boy, the fruit of her womb, suffering as he did, not only physically, but in the crushing of his spirit and hope. Christ's sacrifice was also hers, for he was all she had. As he gave his life so did she.

We talk of the world redeemed by Christ's death; yet as we inspect the world around us it does not look redeemed – quite the opposite! Salvation seems to be a double lock, one of which Christ unlocks by his death, while the other is from our side and is unlocked as we accept the saving work of Christ and assimilate it for ourselves.

Entering the Passion means for us gaining the benefits of the work of Christ. That in effect means healing the relationships that have been broken, the relationship to God, the relationship within ourselves, with others and with creation.

Christ on the cross is the symbol of the joining of heaven and earth, God and humankind. His outstretched arms embrace the whole human race while his upright body stands against the sky like a giant rivet joining heaven and earth. Only God himself could heal the breach between us. We are powerless to do so. It is not we who go upwards to remake the link with God, but God who comes down to do so. The United Nations will never bring peace to the earth without the help of God.

The blood of the cross is a healing balm for the disrupted integrity of our own being. We are wounded and in need of help. Just as in his life Jesus healed those ravaged by disease and disability, and re-integrated the broken lives of the Woman at the Well, and Zacchaeus, so the blood of the cross is healing for us. We can find strength, too, in watching the struggle that took place within Jesus. The Passion is the time when the humanity of Christ is seen in weakness and pain. In Gethsemane he succumbed to a paralysing spate of fear that caused him to cry out to his Father to let him escape. The stress within him was so great that Luke describes his sweat as being like drops of blood falling to the ground. In this lowest point of weakness he appealed for the help and support of his friends, Peter, James and John only to find them asleep. We hesitate to think of Christ as having the human need of companionship and support, because of his divinity, but in the garden he manifestly did need his friends.

His human weakness is shown again on the way to Calvary when three times he fell to the ground. In taking on human nature God was subjecting himself to the limitation and fragility of our kind. In doing so he consecrated it.

Suffering and death have great power to seal and remake bonds between people, families and former enemies. In the case of the Passion of the Lord this re-bonding represents the culmination of what he came to do. At various stages of the Passion we find relationships being remade or strengthened. At other times, however, it was a bonding for evil purpose: Herod and Pilate became friends on Good Friday, but a friendship sealed with the blood of injustice. Yet the encounter with Pilate surely had a deep effect on that Roman Governor, and clearly influenced his wife.

The Way of the Cross is the setting for a series of encounters. Veronica, through an apparently small act of kindness suddenly found that her life was imprinted with the face of Christ, an imprint that would never be erased. Simon of Cyrene, reluctantly yoked to Christ by the cross, is affected to the extent that his sons are later found in the Christian Church.

Other relationships were tested – Peter and the apostles ran away, straining their friendship with Jesus out a of fear of being implicated themselves in his fate, and they had to be brought back and reconciled. Throughout the history of Christianity the cross has proved both bond and test. It is folly. It drains away any pretence or falsification. It makes and breaks friendships as Christ warned that it would do.

The very sight of the crucified brought a healing of relationships. The Centurion was reconciled to the truth and his own part in the injustice caused. ('I have executed a just man.') The Good Thief found healing at this last minute of his life, admitting his guilt and accepting that he was justly punished. In accepting this man Christ reconciled him to himself, to God, and to society. Even at the extremity of death Jesus was concerned with the relationships of humankind. Though his death was a global reconciliation he was nevertheless aware of the needs of individuals. New bonds formed during the passion stand as the symbols of the renewal wrought by Christ's saving death. In consigning Mary to the care of John the Evangelist Jesus says: 'This is YOUR mother, this is YOUR son'. 'Mother' and 'Son' are both relationship words. John stands in the place of Jesus in the place of mankind. Mary becomes our mother.

Forgiveness is conspicuous too, as he wishes forgiveness on the very men who had crucified him, pleading their ignorance. This word of pardon represents a putting into practice of what he had preached to the people as a necessary part of truly fulfilling the law of love. It came to be recognised as the most central teaching of Christ – forgive your enemies. It is a teaching that has scarcely ever been followed. It caused the Jewish leaders to jump to attention since he had touched an area that was highly sensitive – the law. 'You no doubt recognise the saying, An eye for an eye and a tooth for a tooth,' he had said to them, 'but I say to you, no revenge on those who do you wrong, and if someone slaps you on one cheek, turn the other one and let him slap that too! You've heard the saying, love your friends, hate your enemies? Well I'm telling you, love your enemies, and pray for those who oppose you and do you down.'

That was uttered by a teaching Christ of massive strength and authority ('but I say to you...!'); now, on the cross, the teaching is carried out in the midst of degradation.

The restoring of the relationship of humankind to creation is not so easy to see. The elements certainly demonstrated fury at the death of Christ. The violation of Jesus was also the violation of the whole of creation. Darkness came on the earth, the veil in the temple was ripped from top to bottom just as the High Priest had ripped his garment. There was an earthquake, rocks cracked open as did the tombs of the dead. When the covenant with creation is violated, then the results are felt in creation itself. Christ is the centre and meaning of the universe, the cosmic connection between God, humankind, and creation. 'The earth mourns and dies, it languishes and dies, and heaven itself mourns ...for the people have broken the everlasting covenant.' Thus is shown the dire effect of breaking relationship, but Christ's death is the healing salve that creation itself was waiting for: the whole creation is eagerly waiting for God's revelation, and still holds the need for freedom.

Jesus said, 'I am thirsty'. In Christian piety this has always represented his thirst and desire for salvation for all. As saviour and representative of all humankind he thirsts of the unity, rebonding, and healing of all people.

He shouted 'Eloi, Eloi' – 'My God! My God! Why have you deserted me?' He felt that his relationship to the

Father, the very bonding of the Trinity, was being put to the test. That was the relationship from which his whole life derived its strength, the dynamo from which his energy and motivation took source. Did he really doubt his Father's being with him? Part of his acceptance of the human condition was to experience the fragility of trust and the uncertainty of even the strongest strands of our life.

The cross in our lives is accepting what Rahner calls the 'sword of faith'. The sword of faith is any factor which causes disunity or fragmentation within us. As a consequence we strive to live in hope even when we feel that our expectations and our purest aspirations have been shattered. When this shattering seems to have been caused by God himself, or allowed to happen with his connivance, then the sword of faith is tested to the hilt. With Christ we cry out, My God, My God why have you let me down? At such times our lives are anything but havens of peace, calm and trust, but nevertheless they are, at precisely these points, lives of faith. The end of the psalm that Jesus was quoting, whose opening words ('Eloi, Eloi lama sabachthani!') form such a cry of despair is nevertheless optimistic, and Jesus died with the words, 'Into your hands I give my spirit', reasserting the indomitable relationship with the Father in complete abandonment.

Finally, the cross reveals a tremendous truth about God's relationship to us. It is proof of his willingness to go to any length to heal the wounded relationships that we have caused. His healing is a suffering and accepting. God's only answer to Why? is what the Samurai in Endo's novel saw in his wanderings across the world. It was not the number and variety of the nations that struck him but the suffering of the human race that he everywhere met, symbolised and represented by the emaciated figure of Christ on the cross, a figure which the Samurai, as a proud Japanese, would have despised before he became a Christian.

*Texts to help your prayer of the passion:*

Isaiah 52:13 – 53 end: Song of the Suffering Servant
Mark 15: The Passion
John 18:33-40: The title of Jesus, INRI
Luke 23:34,42-43,46; John 19:25-27,28-29,30; Matthew
27:46-47: Words from the Cross

# CHAPTER 8

# 'God Endlessly Giving'

## The Resurrection

The Passion can be seen as waste, the giving of love which is not reciprocated, but instead is turned on the lover. It is frustration and souring of relationships, the ultimate act of severance. Yet, to use another image, God the painter who finds that the picture is going wrong yet manages to produce the final masterpiece. There was a time when God was tempted to destroy his attempt at creation and start again when He looked at the evil in the world and regretted he had made humankind.

But where the crucifixion was the frustration of God's love, the Resurrection is the triumph of it. Easter is a celebration of God's life in the world, the affirmation of the bond of love.

The Resurrection narratives are a strange collection of events, the frustration of exegetes or those who wish to have things neatly tied up. There is confusion of place and time. It is difficult to decipher exactly what happened when. It's a case of 'now you see me, now you don't.'

If there is one thread going through this time between the Resurrection and Ascension it is that of building up again the relationships and bonds that had worn thin or been broken. In the fourth week of the Spiritual Exercises St Ignatius refers to the risen Christ as a bringer of Consolation. Where the crucifixion could be seen as the work of the Evil One, breaking the threads of life and union, so the Resurrection can be seen as the work of the Good Spirit, re-establishing life and relationship.

First and foremost the Risen Christ had to reassure his friends that he was alive and with them. Yet that life was a risen, a renewed life, not the same as it had been in the days of his public ministry when they had roamed the hillsides of Galilee together. So at one and the same time he was saying to his disciples when he appeared to them, 'Look, I am here, I am real, I am Me, but I am different. I have overcome once and for all the destructive forces that dissolve relationships.'

To establish that he was real he invited them to touch him, to see that he was not a ghost; and indeed to poke about in the wounds which signified who he was – the person who had hung on the cross. When all other proof seemed to fail he asked for something to eat. The disappearance of the food would seem to clinch the matter!

To establish that he was different he paid scant attention to the laws of physics, batting in and out of locked rooms and coming and going with total freedom. Not an indiscriminate coming and going to be sure, always it moved to remake that which was broken, whether confidence, faith, or love. Mary Magdalene sat disconsolate, the centre of her life removed to such an extent that there was not even a body to reverence. God had once saved her in Jesus, now God had abandoned her again. The corner-stone of her new life had been removed and the whole edifice had collapsed. So Jesus came to rebuild what had fallen.

When praying in the resurrection it is good to try to use contemplation of the imaginative kind. It is a matter not just of reflecting on the events of the Resurrection but of going to meet Jesus, or being present when he comes to meet you.

Place yourself in the Upper Room in John (20:19) and sense the atmosphere of the room after the crucifixion. What are they all waiting for? Sense the desolation, which is the absence of Jesus. Sense the despair of the disciples, witnessed to by pointless activity, wandering up and down...

108

then suddenly, Jesus stands in the middle of the room. The atmosphere changes, desolation gives way to consolation. See the wounds in his hands and feet, hear his message of peace.

Again, walk on the road to Emmaus (Lk 24), with the two disciples, escaping from that heavy atmosphere, convinced that it was all over and they could go back home to pick up their lives. Yet their minds, thoughts, their whole BEING was back there in Jerusalem, with Christ. You too share the heaviness of their thoughts. Like them, you pay scant attention to the stranger who comes alongside. With them you pour out the story of the would-be Saviour who now was dead. Then listen as he brings enlightenment and hope and new joy. He didn't tell them anything new. THEY told HIM the history, and he referred them to the Scriptures they knew only too well. He used their experience and knowledge. Let him use yours as you pray.

In that walk Jesus did several things. He renewed his own relationship with them so that they became reunited in the name of Father, Son and Spirit. He fulfilled that role of Renewer for all those he came to in the resurrection, renewing his own relationship with them. Where unfaithfulness had fractured the bond, as in the case of Peter, there was a special and deep reconciliation. On the shore of Lake Tiberias he asked Peter three times if he loved him, bound him to himself with a triple tie. In doing so he reassured us all that it is never he, Jesus, who has been delinquent, but we. He has never moved an inch from us.

Those two disciples going to Emmaus found that their lives had been re-established in trust and faith and this had brought a new integration. Their inner selves gained a cohesion and wholeness which would remain with them. Facets of their lives fell into place, a new meaning held them together.

The effect on the two was to integrate their lives and their own selves. It renewed their self esteem, and individual worth. No longer would they drag their heels away from Jerusalem! We might spend fruitful time thinking back over the resurrections in our own lives, when we had felt broken, when we were down and exhausted, without hope or love. Perhaps we too went from Jerusalem and the wreckage of our relationship to Christ. Without our knowing it he caught up with us on the road, opened the Scriptures to us, set our hearts burning and then, in the very place where we had thought to evade him he was voluptuously present!

There are often clear steps in this recovery. A first and basic one is to recognise how we are, acknowledging that we are down, desperate, suicidal, in need of help. We have to allow our fault, our inadequacy and step out of the whirlpool in order to let God tell us over again that he has not stopped loving us.

With this new faith and integration came new energy on the road to Emmaus. No doubt it was spiritual but it certainly overflowed into every crevice of their lives. They say that Emmaus is 7 miles from Jerusalem and you feel they were dragging their heels disconsolately on the way; yet they returned posthaste! A new buoyancy, a new spirit had taken them over. Tillich wrote that there are three fundamental anxieties that threaten the well-being of the human race. The first is the anxiety of meaningless, the second the anxiety of fate and death, and the third the anxiety of sin and damnation. Given a rooted faith in Christ these three anxieties can be, if not removed, at least clothed in hope. The two on the road to Emmaus moved from a state of meaningless wandering to a new purposefulness. The man walking with them on the road was a sign of the defeat of the sting of death since he accompanies us through it; and he is the very sign of forgiveness which counters the anxiety of sin.

The Resurrection is not an isolated event but the initiation of an era, a new age of God's reign. The work of healing of the broken must go on throughout time. The Risen Christ's main role was to re-establish relationships that were broken or fallen into disrepair. And that is the work of the Spirit in the new age: the Go-between God establishes connection, renews relationship to the Father, brings back the Prodigal. It is the work of re-creation.

The Resurrection is about Transformation of that which is dead into that which is living. Contemplating the gospels enables us to see that change quite clearly in the disciples. The group in the Upper Room before the Lord appeared, the two disciples on the road to Emmaus, show the effects of desolation and despair. Zest and motivation have disappeared from their lives, they are listless, harking back to the past only to see what might have been. Their inclination is backward-looking, not forward. They fail to live the present.

When the Risen Lord appeared all that changed. They became full of enthusiasm and energy. What is particularly noticeable for us as we contemplate is that this enthusiasm and joy did not disappear when Jesus returned to his Father at the ascension. The gospel of Luke tells us that they returned to Jerusalem rejoicing (Lk 24:52). At once they began to discuss the replacement for Judas in their number (Acts 1). There is now no sign of depression or 'what do we do now?'

To reinforce this sense of purpose and joy, contemplate the scene of the cure of the beggar at the Beautiful Gate of the Temple (Acts 3:1-10). A beggar sitting at the gate saw Peter and John going into the Temple and appealed to them for alms. Without hesitation, it seems, Peter fixed him with a gaze, and said, 'I have no silver or gold but what I have I give you! In the name of Jesus of Nazareth, walk!' and he grabbed his arm and pulled him to his feet and watched him hop about in joy. This is not the action or the word of a man who is depressed and feeling that the friend and master of his life is dead and gone. He was totally conscious of the power and presence of Jesus, acting in and through himself.

It was through their experience of the Christ present in power and spirit that Peter and the disciples, and especially Paul, came to a realisation of a Christ who now stood with his Father in glory yet who was with them as they worked for the kingdom on earth. Christ had become for them the Lord and Master of Creation. When we look at Jesus what do we see? Ask your average Catholic (if there is such a being!) who Jesus was. 'The Son of God (or just, God), the Saviour who saved us by his death on the cross.' He is a Red Adair come to cap the burning oil-well and put out the fire of sin. If the well had not gone on fire there would have been no need for Adair!

To suggest that there might have been another way of seeing Christ seems unacceptable to some. Yet in St Paul's letter to the Colossians you read:

He is the true icon,
the visible image of the God we cannot see,
the First-born of all creation;
for in him were created
all things, in heaven and on the earth,
all that we can see, and all we cannot see –
all were created through him and for him.
He existed before all these things
and he holds them all together,
bonded in him...

So there are two ways of seeing the 'purpose' of Christ's coming:

As Saviour, come because the world is in a mess.
As Lord of Creation who would have come anyway.

To see Jesus' purpose solely as rescuer seems to allow our sinfulness to dictate God's plans. Christ is redeemer, certainly, but he is more than that. He is the centre of the whole created universe. He is the centre of our religion in a much wider way than the person who lived in history, a short life with a brutal end. In time and beyond time. Everything was made for him, as though the Father created it all as a birthday present for his son!

That which was there from the beginning,
which we have heard with our very ears
and seen with our own eyes,
and watched and touched with our own hands –
this very Word of Life is our subject;
for this Word of Life was made visible.

In such sense-words did John the Apostle talk of the love that God had for the world, a love so great that he sent his Son. 'You are heir, my Son, go to my vineyard. Be for me there. Be the visible sign of my presence, my promise, my love.'

Yet still we suspect God of stealing in the back door in disguise, pretending to be human. We peer through his humanity intent on seeing the wonder-worker of heaven, rather than the embodiment of God on earth. Did not God intend us to look at a man, Jesus, because there we find, in the Son, the image of the Father? 'This is my beloved Son in whom I am well pleased. Listen to him!' See him too, touch him. God wants to be embodied so that he can be seen and touched, and all we do is try to look through him to find a ghostly God. We are to work from Jesus to God, not the other way about. Let's get our horses and carts in the right order! That is our privilege as created beings, to work with that which is material.

Incarnation is at the centre of our religion. The Coming is not one of grudging necessity but one of desire. Not a God frowning at what he sees and exclaiming, 'Oh God, look at that mess, I'd better go and do something about it!', but a Father sending his son and heir to go and take possession of their land.

Even as Rescuer the coming was not reluctant or forced. In a wonderful poem R.S. Thomas tells of God the Father showing the world to the Son, with its griefs and shadows and the sufferings of its people; and the Son answering, 'Let me go there...' 'Let me!' He wants to go there. It is an expression of desire not duty. He wants to be with his own people, wants to be here with us. Surely that is the message of Advent. This was no reluctant coming. God moves towards embodiment.

God has no horror of the world he made. When Augustine wrote that he did not 'abhor the virgin's womb' at his coming there is the implication that he should have abhorred it. It was a divine condescension to come. Yet St John says that God loved the world so much that he sent his son... Dualistic thoughts lurk around our way of thinking of God and the world. They seek to drive a wedge between God and creation, not in the sense that God inevitably transcends and outdistances creation, but in the sense that God and the world are ineradicably opposed, since one is good and the other evil. If God is to come into this world of ours it is with extreme reluctance and with a view only to rescue us from its clutches.

The letter to the Colossians shows us a different picture. This Christ is the centre and meaning of Creation. Creation is for him. It is like a royal ball in the palace, the music is playing and the people are assembled, but it is when the Royal Couple arrive and set it in motion that it gains its full impetus.

That is why Peter in Acts 4:12 declared to the crowd: 'For of all the names in the world given to us, this is the only one by which we can be saved...' Through the ages the Church has held to this, at first rigidly and without compromise even until the Second Vatican Council. It led to an intolerance which we find difficult to accept today and to the zeal of men like St Francis Xavier who made such heroic efforts to baptise those whom they seemed to think would be condemned otherwise. As the world was more explored and better known it became apparent that the majority of people on earth were thus condemned to hell because Christians were in the minority. Much earlier the problem had arisen of what to do about those who died before the coming of Christ, especially unbaptized babies.

Perhaps if we see Christ in St Paul's way, as the centre and meaning of creation, we need not be so circumscribed in our way of thinking. Christ is at the centre whether or not we can acknowledge it. And Christ is at work throughout the fabric of the world, permeating it with his spirit. It isn't only in our church that he is found, nor only in our baptismal font that his grace is given. He is not confined to our statement of the creed, nor is his truth circumscribed by our dogmatic statements. When told that others were preaching using his name Jesus was glad and said, 'Who is not against me is with me.' We have been inclined to say, 'Who is not with us is against us.' Where his statement was inclusive, ours tends to be exclusive.

This way of seeing Christ, as Firstborn of Creation, serves to reinforce the sense of God being immanent in creation itself. However we act in the world for the building up of the kingdom we are acting in Christ. His overall position will have a profound effect on the way I view the world and all other people in it, and that will include those of other ways of thinking to my own. 'Firstborn' is a word that implies the presence of brothers and sisters. Christ is the firstborn, we are part of the family. When any person acts out of love for another, when a person in India brings comfort and support to his dying mother, or a wife visits her husband in prison in Russia, they are fulfilling Christ's purpose whether or not they are Christian. When warring leaders come together to try to establish peace and equity in the world they are acting in a Christlike way. When a person listens to the radio and hears a surge of music and sits enraptured, determined to hear that music again, I'm sure it doesn't really matter that they do not know that it is by Beethoven. All that matters is that they hear his genius, appreciate his music. So too with Christ – I'm sure he is not worried whether people formally use his name, as long as they fulfil his meaning.

In coming into our world Jesus is telling us about the Father. He tells us that his Father is 'Abba', not distanced but close. He tells us that the nature of that Father is to be in relationship. The very word 'father' is a relationship word. You cannot be a father, or a mother, unless you have a child. God is revealed by Jesus as a threesome.

Jesus said to them: 'No one can go to the Father, except through me. Knowing me you know my Father too, now you have seen me you have seen him too.'

'Let's see the Father, it's all we need,' said Philip.

'Oh dear!' sighed Jesus. 'How long have I been with you, and you don't even know me yet! I've told you, if you've seen me you've seen the Father, so how can you be asking to see him? Don't you believe that I am in the Father and the Father is in me? Don't you see that? Can't you understand that the things I say, the things I do, I'm not doing them of myself, they are the work of the Father in me.'

He couldn't really have made it clearer. God's very being is to be in relationship. John said the same thing again when he said that God is love. Loving is outward to another. The Father's very being is expressed in the Son and the Spirit. Yet the Father is his own person.

It's the same strange paradox that we feel within ourselves. We want to be individual and strong within ourselves, integrated. At the same time, we know that our being is expressed by love, by going out to others. In fact, that very integration that we seek within ourselves can only be achieved in and through our love for other people. Yet we are individuals, and must be. In other words, we are reflecting, in our own selves, the way God is. We are in his image and likeness.

Further on in the same chapter 14 of John Jesus shows how this 'in-othering' of the Father spreads out into creation.

'Then you'll realise that I am in my Father, and that you are in me, and I am in you.' Creation is the Father's love uniting the whole through Jesus.

Jesus did not come reluctantly, but to his own family. He showed us what God is like, that Abba he referred to. If we really believe this we have to acknowledge that God comes to us as a servant, who doesn't want us to kow-tow to him, he wants to be our servant. He consistently put aside position and honour and status in life and preferred both poverty and ordinariness for ten-elevenths of his life! Above all, Christ shows us that God is a God of compassion, at one with the sufferings of his people.

An expression of Christ's burning desire to be and to stay with us is found in Luke's account of the Last Supper which is introduced by Jesus' saying, 'I have longed and longed to eat this Passover with you...' It is an emphatic way of expressing the depth of his desire, literally, 'With desire have I desired...' Then, during the meal he instituted the sacrament of the Eucharist. Our great familiarity with this sacrament and the fact that it takes up such an everyday function as eating have perhaps blurred this extraordinary sign that has meanings and emphases that are practically endless. It has always been seen as a memorial of the passion, in the separation of the body and blood. The symbolism of the food, the manna of the desert, is also strongly represented. But there is a cosmic element of the Eucharist that is not so often stressed. The Eucharist is an act of love between God and his universe through the mediation of man in Christ.

It is an act. Jesus commanded us to do something, not just think about it. 'Take, Eat!' It is blunt and earthy. Eating is a basic animal activity. Often people will say in confession that they have had unworthy thoughts, even impure ones, during Mass and even as they go up to Communion. They may even be put off going to Communion because they don't 'feel' right. But the command is not to feel right or even think right. It is to DO. And the thing we have to do is Eat. As the German saying has it, 'A person is what he eats.' Our being is what we eat. Being is dependent on the body. Through that very material activity of swallowing material food into our material bodies we receive life. It is this very activity that Christ has made the medium through which his life is communicated. We are what we eat. And what we eat is Christ.

By taking the bread and wine of the Eucharist we enter into the life of Christ, become part of his body. In this way we enter too into that act of love of God for his universe. Christ is the Firstborn of creation. By entering into him, becoming part of his body we enter into the mystery of creation. Thereby we enter the nerve-ganglion of the universe.

I have spoken of relationship to others, our fellow men and women. Can we speak in the same way of a relationship to Christ? Christians are told so often how important it is, that our life has to be rooted in Christ, not just in our dealings with our neighbour, but in direct contact with him. Is it realistic to speak in these terms, of a personal relationship to a man we have never met but read about in a gospel, who died 2000 years ago? Is it not fiction, or fantasy? Can a woman, for instance, still retain a relationship with a husband who has been dead for ten years? It is a real question.

I can only say that I am convinced it is possible because it does happen. Christ is no ordinary person. His being spans time and space. The Risen Christ of the gospels

118

reassured the disciples that he was real and present and would continue to be so for them, though no longer visible. Though lacking the visible reassurance of most human relationships the unity with Christ is formed both by him and by us. It may go through stages of development from an early, more excited time, to a more down to earth, pedestrian form. In later years, as in a marriage, there may not be much left to say, but each is present to the other, like an old married couple sitting opposite each other by the fire, he smoking his pipe and reading the paper, she knitting (to use two usual stereotypes!), but neither saying much. Yet what a difference if one of them were not there! Each is present to the other.

The final part of the Spiritual Exercises of Ignatius is 'The Contemplation to Deepen the Love of God'. It is a consecration of ourselves and our capabilities and faculties to God. We invite God in to sanctify our perceptions so that we can see the world with God's eyes, as it were.

The 'Contemplatio' as it is often called, begins with a brief reminder that love is expressed in what we do rather than what we say. The son in the gospel who says 'no' to his father when asked to go and work in the field, but then goes, expresses more love than the one who says 'yes' enthusiastically, and then does not go. We are then asked, imaginatively, to see ourselves standing before the whole court of heaven! For many of us this can be a daunting place to stand! We can just see them all frowning at us and wagging fingers. Ignatius is not seeing it in that way at all. More like emerging from the tunnel at Wembley as one of the players on Cup Final day. A great roar of applause! Our friends and supporters and family are all there, supporting us.

The first point of the contemplation is to bring to mind all that I can be grateful for, first of all globally, looking around at the world I live in, the earth, the things that grow and breathe, the trees and skies and all the support systems that interact to keep the cosmos going. All those support systems keep me going, despite the fact that I often work to their detriment and destruction! All those systems, in fact, that the human animal seems determined to destroy! I allow my sense of wonder full play as I wander round the cosmos, gazing and praising the instigator of all this. We are encouraged to think back to our days of biology at school and see that 'pyramid of life' with forms of life growing more specialised and complicated as we rise up the triangle until at the pinnacle we find the human being at that special point of contact with God.

I then dwell on the many gifts I have received in my own life, everything, all the circumstances of my birth and home and country, the food and clothes I have taken so much for granted, education, and above all the love I have received.

Then too I remember that God sent his Son. I allow full play again to the wonder of that mystery. In a word Ignatius is inviting us to open out all the channels of thankfulness in ourselves so as to be more aware of the work of God in our world.

This exercise of the Contemplatio can in fact be done after I finish retreat. It is a formula for proceeding with my life. It is the Risen Lord who is with me as I go out of retreat, it is he who is present to me in my prayer, he who is present to me in the Eucharist, and he who talks to me, touches me, embraces me in my neighbour.

*To help my praying at the end of retreat*

1. I ask myself if Christ is the centre of my life? What does he mean to me? Contemplate again Mark 8:27-30. See and hear Jesus ask the group (including myself) 'Who do people say I am?' and hear what they reply. Then he

looks at me and asks, 'And you, Mary (or Jean, or Jimmy, or John, or Margaret...) who do YOU say I am?' Try to answer sincerely for yourself to Jesus.

2. Pray using the image of the Vine (John 15:5-17) and see that Jesus is the centre and meaning of the whole ramification of life and cosmos. Get the sense of being part of that plant, and depending for life on the sap that flows from the stem.

3. Colossians 1:15-20: The icon of the Father
4. John 1:1-18: The word became flesh
5. Acts 4:8-12: By this name and no other
6. 1 Corinthians 11:17-34: The Eucharist

# THE HEART IS A SACRED SPACE

Pamela Hayes

This reflection takes up a pilgrim stance in search of the space of the heart, allowing the mystics and prophets to mingle with psychotherapists and a whole variety of seekers along its borderland.

It discovers that the heart is not only a psychological sign of human vulnerability but a powerful symbol of a theological reality. This is because we can see in the wounded heart of Christ, an image of God that a world, aware of its own brokenness, can receive. There, all at once, is the anguish of humanity and the compassion of God loving us towards the wholeness of being human. In Jesus, the heart is truly sacred. But what is actual in him points towards a truth still to be realised in every human being: that the heart is a sacred space. The hope for all creation at the dawn of the twenty-first century lies in rediscovering this truth.

*Sr Pamela Hayes is a member of the Society of the Sacred Heart. After many years in Higher Education lecturing in Religious Studies, she is now involved in spiritual direction and retreats and in forming others for this ministry.*

208 pages          085439 493 1

# THE KINGDOM OF GOD IS LIKE…

## Thomas Keating

The most vivid and enduring messages in the Gospels are found in the parables and sayings of Jesus. Packed into these short stories are clues about the meaning of life, the nature of God, and the purpose of creation. But sometimes their very familiarity causes the modern reader to slide too easily past the message and meaning.

In *The Kingdom of God is Like…* Thomas Keating stirs the imagination with his insightful commentary on the parables. Although originally told to people in a vastly different world, these stories are timeless and have much to say to today's readers. As Fr Keating says, 'When rightly understood, the parables help us to see how extraordinary a wisdom teacher Jesus really was and how revolutionary, in the best sense of the word, was the content of what he taught and to whcih he bore witness by his life and death.

*THOMAS KEATING is a Cistercian monk and former abbot of St Joseph's Abbey in Spencer, Massachusetts, and is known to thousands of Christians as a founder of the Centering Prayer movement.*

118 pages          085439 463 X                    £4.95

# EYES ON THE LORD

## Duncan Basil

Duncan Basil is a priest who has been over forty years a
Cistercian monk in Europe and Africa, working at every
monastic job from growing tomatoes, keeping bees to
binding books. As a layman he flew for nine years in the
Royal Air Force, serving in squadrons in the Middle East
and the Mediterranean in the Second World War. Then for
two years he read English Literature at university before
asking to enter his present abbey.

This book, the fruit of that diverse experience, is based on
talks given to retreatants and religious communities over the
years. As a contemplative with vivid experience of the
active life both past and present (which he calls the average
mayhem of a monastery), he is able to show with a relaxed
but stimulating clarity how both ways, whether they overlap
or diverge, can bring us home provided we keep our eyes on
the Lord.

94 pages          085439 476 1

# MARTHA AND MARY
## Meeting Christ as Friend
### Anastasio Ballestrero

These meditations in simple language are an invitation to relive the Christian mystery by looking at some aspects of meeting with Christ.

In the house of Martha, Mary and Lazarus, Christ is with friends. Martha represents the concrete realities of the Incarnation, Mary the realization that Christ is the Word of God. Both tell us something about receiving in love and friendship the Lord's visit to our house so as to serve him and bear witness to him, the Saviour of humanity and the world.

A fresh look at the ways of prayer, this book – addressed primarily to consecrated persona – invites us to welcome the Lord as friend, to talk to and be with him as friends do. Nothing is more important than to remain with him.

*Anastasio Ballestrero, a Carmelite and former Cardinal Archbishop of Turin.*

125 pages          ISBN 085439 483 4